101 Ways to Love Your Grandkids

Bob&Emilie Barnes

HARVEST HOUSE PUBLISHERS

EUGENE, OREGON

Cover by Terry Dugan Design, Minneapolis, Minnesota

101 WAYS TO LOVE YOUR GRANDKIDS
Copyright © 2004 by Bob and Emilie Barnes
Published by Harvest House Publishers
Eugene, Oregon 97402

Select devotions are adapted from the following:
Minute Meditations for Healing and Hope © 2003 by Emilie Barnes
Minute Meditations for Men © 1998 by Bob Barnes
15 Minutes Alone with God © 1994 by Emilie Barnes
The Spirit of Loveliness © 1992 by Emilie Barnes

Library of Congress Cataloging-in-Publication Data

Barnes, Bob, 1933-
    101 ways to love your grandkids / Bob Barnes and Emilie Barnes.
        p. cm.
    Includes bibliographical references.
    ISBN 0-7369-1376-9 (pbk.)
    1. Grandparents—Prayer-books and devotions—English.   I. Title: One hundred and one ways to love your grandkids.   II. Title: One hundred one ways to love your grandkids.
III. Barnes, Emilie. IV. Title.
    BV4845.B37 2004
    248.8'45—dc22   2004001047

Printed in the United States of America

04   05   06   07   08   09   10   11   / BP-MS /   10   9   8   7   6   5   4   3   2   1

Dedication

This book is dedicated to all the grandparents who feel led to actively give and model love for their grandchildren. There are those who say, "I've done my job in raising our children. Now they can raise their own children, while Mom and I do our own thing."

Then there are others, like you, who feel that God is leading you to help shape the lives of these grandchildren that God has given you. You want to help instill those values you cherish so much in these small children.

You are passing on your legacy to many future generations. You are saying, "Not my will be done but, God, Your will be done in our lives." One set of grandparents wants to go the selfish way, but you are willing to make the sacrifices that are necessary to raise healthy adults.

This book is dedicated to the selfless grandparents who desire to make an impact on the next generation.

We have five grandchildren, and we would not trade one of our sacrificial moments for our own desires. We thank the Lord daily for these young lives. They are ready to face the world on their own two feet. We can look back and say,

"We had an impact here, and we have had an impact there." What a legacy! The grandchildren will never forget the part that their Grammy Em and PaPa Bob had in their lives.

May you, too, have the same impact on the grandchildren that God has blessed you with.

—PaPa Bob and Grammy Em

The closest friends I have made all through life have been people who also grew up close to a loved and loving grandfather and grandmother.

MARGARET MEAD

Contents

Introduction

Grandparents have a long history of being teachers to their children and to their grandchildren. In 2 Timothy 1:5 NASB, Paul states, "For I am mindful of the sincere faith within you, which first dwelt in your grandmother Lois and your mother Eunice."

We as grandparents have a great opportunity to teach our grandchildren traditions, truths, and values that their parents may overlook or not have time for. Because of the various complexities of today's society and family values, we can provide spiritual training when the grandchildren are with us.

With plenty of ideas, activities, devotions, meditations, words of encouragement, and Scriptures, this book is really an anthology for grandparenting. We have designed these meditations to be read by grandparents as a couple, but they are also wonderful for anyone to read alone. However, if you are a couple, consider discussing each of the 101 ways to love your grandkids. It becomes easier to raise this second set of children when PaPa and Grammy are on the same page spiritually.

The four sections allow you to focus on the main legacies grandparents are able to pass on to their children's children:

+ "The Legacy of Memories" overflows with simple ideas, prayers, and stories to encourage your sharing of time, self, and creativity. Each moment you spend with a child is an opportunity to create or share a wonderful memory.

+ "The Legacy of Faith" provides tools to create this significant foundation. There is nothing greater than the gift of belief and hope.

+ "The Legacy of Life" inspires you to integrate your faith with daily living so you can be an example at all times.

+ "The Legacy of Love" is filled with ways to show you care and to model the Father's unconditional love.

May you find this book a very valuable tool in assisting the raising and nurturing of your grandchildren. You are so very important in helping to mold who they will become.

How to Create a Prayer Journal

We know that any grandparent reading this is a praying grandparent...or is desiring to become one. So we encourage you to round up a notebook and a favorite pen and start a prayer journal. As you make your way through these 101 ways to love your grandkids, you will be inspired and instructed to pray.

To keep your heart and mind on your grandchildren as you pray, place a photo of each child in the notebook pocket, or in clear insert sleeves, or on the divider pages.

Personalize your journal with your favorite Scriptures, quotes, or thoughts about grandparenting. While you are gleaning ideas about grandparenting, you will also begin to recall your own stories, examples, and sources of inspiration. Often your stories will be the examples of prayers answered.

Make entries in your notebook each time you pray. Put the date, time, and your location on the top line. List any Scripture or quote you might be reflecting on before you pray. Write out your prayers for each grandchild and those for yourself.

Create a list of praises for that day. How is God blessing you as a grandparent?

Leave room for future notes. When a prayer is answered, write down the date and references about how God worked in that situation. Even if you do not do this part, we guarantee that as you revisit your prayer journal a month from now...a year from now...five years from now, you will see how many of these prayers were answered in amazing ways.

Pray throughout a grandchild's life. Consider it a privilege of this time in your life. You have the time, the wisdom, and the heart to be committed to a rich prayer life. Use this gift to bathe your grandchildren and your children in prayer daily.

The physical image of the finished notebooks piling up over the years will be a visual reminder of God's faithfulness and His presence in the life of your family.

Grandparent's Legacy Prayer

Father God, give me the strength and vision to pray regularly for my grandchildren. Hear my prayers as I express my concerns and my praises. May I look to Your Word for inspiration and support. I want to be the best grandparent I can be, Lord. When I am with my grandchildren, may I show them Your love. And may I express my own love by giving them over to You in prayer.

Work in the hearts of my children so they become strong, wise parents. Lead me to be a helper. Keep me from being critical. Let my experience and patience serve them. Tug at my heart when I should be more sensitive to their needs as well as the needs of the grandchildren. Help me to be aware always of how I can be a godly example and servant for my family.

Thank You for this role of grandparent and for this journey. I look forward to the plans You have for me and my family. May I open my hands and life to all that You want to give to me. Let me be a faithful steward of the gifts you have given to me. When I face my own trials, let the surrounding blessings remind me of my heritage of faith.

I ask for Your guidance, compassion, and strength as I offer to my grandchildren the legacies of memories, faith, life, and love.

Amen.

The Legacy
of Memories

Memories

Do you know what is so exciting about the legacy of memories? Memories require an investment of yourself. If you share a personal memory, you are revealing a part of your life to your grandchild. If you are creating a memory *with* a grandchild, you are interacting, communicating, or just "being" with that child. Both scenarios provide a chance for you to have a stronger, more intimate relationship with another generation in your family.

Never hold back the urge to share a story from your past. And do not ever resist the desire to pick up the phone and call your grandchild. Each is an offering of a memory and is truly priceless.

In this first portion of the book, you will find activities and ideas interspersed with devotions. We want to get you started with plenty of material and inspiration. Hopefully you will be encouraged by our personal journey and the things we have learned. All grandparents experience the trials and joys of growing older and wiser. Exciting moments in your life are still to come, and grandchildren will be a part of many of those moments. As your journey continues, your gathering of memories continues. We want you to make sweet, sweet memories with the wonderful children in your life.

May these "ways to love your grandkids" enrich your days spent with these delightful beings. And remember, just as those children are a gift to you, *you* are a gift to them. So never stop giving.

1

Memories on the garden bench.

I thank my God every time I remember you.

PHILIPPIANS 1:3

It was a warm, sunny day for January in Riverside, California. Two of our five grandchildren were helping us enjoy this fine day. Ten-and-a-half-year-old Christine was helping her Grammy Em plan and cook the dinner. She was picking flowers to arrange for our dinner table. PaPa Bob and Bevan were raking the garden and picking oranges, avocados, and lemons off our trees that surround our property.

As the afternoon progressed, our working men became warm and tired.

Christine said, "Grammy, let's have tea." That is all it takes for me to stop whatever I am doing and put the kettle on for Christine and me to have tea. In the process, we poured the men a tall glass of fresh juice on ice and prepared some yummy-for-the-tummy snacks. We carried the treats up the hill to PaPa and Bevan. How happy they were to receive the refreshment. They thanked us and headed for the bench that sits under a large, shady avocado tree overlooking the grounds and our quaint, tree-lined little Rumsey Drive which winds by our barn.

As Christine and I left them, we headed back toward the house. Christine took my hand and said, "Grammy, I love you." "I love you, too, Christine," I said.

I prepared the tea kettle, and Christine pulled down the teapot and put the teacups on the table with our special silver teaspoons. We toasted thick sourdough bread that we spread with jam and butter. It was an instant tea party—just Christine and me.

That night as my Bob and I crawled in bed, we began to share about our day with the oh-so-wonderful grandchildren.

"What do a PaPa and seven-year-old grandson talk about on the bench under the big avocado tree?" I asked.

"Oh, very special things," Bob replied. "Boys talk just like you girls talk."

I could still picture PaPa Bob and seven-year-old Bevan—with smudges of dirt on both their faces—sitting on that bench.

Bob continued, "I told Bevan, 'Someday, Bevan, when PaPa's in heaven and you drive down Rumsey Drive as a man, you'll look at this bench we are sitting on and you can remember the day Grammy Em and sister Christine served us jam and toast with a glass of juice.' Then Bevan said, 'Not only will I remember, but I will bring my son and someday he will bring his son and point to the bench and tell him about the toast and jam we ate on the bench under that big avocado tree over there.'"

How does a little boy understand and think through the process of generations?

How blessed we are to have the God-given opportunity to teach our children and grandchildren about the beauty of God's creations, about life and death, and most of all about God the Father, God the Son, and God the Holy Spirit.

2

Share your testimony.

He said to them, "Go into all the world and preach the good news to all creation."

MARK 16:15

Share with your grandchildren about how you came to the Lord. If possible, give a date when this great event occurred. One of the great thrills of life is encouraging your grandchildren to accept Jesus as their own personal Savior.

Use your prayer journal to first write out your testimony if you have not ever done that. Do not worry if it is a simple journey or if it involves hard times. God uses every kind of spiritual story to show His love and mercy. Your memory of first meeting the Lord should be a memory you are eager to share with your grandchild.

Go into the world to share the good news, but first share with your family!

3

Know what you are building.

Two stonecutters were asked what they were doing. The first one said, "I'm cutting this stone into blocks." The second replied, "I'm on a team that's building a cathedral." When you spend time with your grandchildren or take time to communicate with them, understand them, and create memories...you are building lives. Each stone you cut and position is creating a bigger structure. Your efforts today will help shape the future of the special people in your family.

4
Memorize comforting words.

It will serve you and your grandchildren well if you memorize some Scriptures of comfort and have them do the same. Many times in growing children's lives—and throughout their adulthood—God's words of peace and hope will circle back through their minds and offer great comfort.

As we get older, it is difficult to face the idea that we will not always be around to provide the comfort or the words of encouragement. But your legacy will live on in the hearts of other people when you take the time to share God's wisdom. Start with these Scriptures and keep adding on:

> I urge you to live a life worthy of the calling you have received. Be completely humble and gentle; be patient, bearing with one another in love.
>
> EPHESIANS 4:1-2

> Do not be anxious about anything, but in everything, by prayer and petition, with thanksgiving, present your requests to God.
>
> PHILIPPIANS 4:6

> I wait for the LORD, my soul waits, and in his word I put my hope. My soul waits for the Lord more than watchmen wait for the morning.
>
> PSALM 130:5-6

I will refresh the weary and satisfy the faint.

JEREMIAH 31:25

Are not five sparrows sold for two pennies? Yet not one of them is forgotten by God. Indeed, the very hairs of your head are all numbered. Don't be afraid; you are worth more than many sparrows.

LUKE 12:6-7

Have mercy on me, O God, according to your unfailing love; according to your grcat compassion blot out my transgressions....Wash me, and I will be whiter than snow.

PSALM 51:1,7

5
Make bedtime special.

Ah, bedtime! The grandchildren have played hard, had a filling dinner, taken a warm bath or shower, dressed in their pajamas, and prepared for bed.

This is the relaxing time, the cooling-down period of the day, just before they fall asleep for a good night's rest. The easiest thing to do is shuffle them off to bed with a good-night kiss and a possible short "Now I lay me down to sleep" prayer. But if you hastily put them to bed, you miss an opportunity to establish a great legacy that will last all their lives. You can impart so much in this short period of time.

Whether you sing with the grandchildren, pray, or share a story, you are creating very special memories in those children's lives.

6
Say bedtime prayers.

Saying bedtime prayers is a wonderful way to encourage a personal conversation with God. If you are lucky enough to host your grandchildren for an overnight stay, this time of prayer gives you an opportunity to share God and create a meaningful tradition.

You can help these youngsters realize the power of prayer. Share how God has been with you throughout your lifetime. Share instances where God has said, "yes," "no," and "not yet."

Impress on these young hearts that God hears all of our prayers, but He does not always answer them on our timetable. God's clock is much bigger than our little watch.

There will be times when these grandchildren will want to pray their own prayers. Theirs can be short or long, silent or audible, free-style or written. As grandparents, use this precious time to pray with your grandchild. Nothing is more heartwarming than to see and hear a grandparent and their grandchild praying together.

Model while they are young, and they will more likely model what you did as they get older.

Here are some prayers to consider sharing with your special grandchild:

May the Lord, mighty God, bless and keep you forever. Grant you peace, perfect peace, courage in every endeavor. Lift up your eyes and see His face, and His grace forever. May the Lord, mighty God, bless and keep you forever.

TRADITIONAL

O God, who givest us not only the day for labor and the night for rest, but also the peace of this blessed day; grant, we beseech Thee, that its quiet may be profitable to us in heavenly things, and refresh and strengthen us to finish the work which Thou hast given us to do; through Jesus Christ our Lord. Amen.

JAMES MARTINEAU

As the evening falls, dear Lord, and while I seek Your face in prayers, grant me the joy of good friends, the creative power of new interests, and the peace of a quiet heart. As darkness comes grant me light to judge the errors and the wisdom of the day's work. And grant me again the healing touch of sleep. Amen.

AUTHOR UNKNOWN

I thank Thee, Father, for the way Thy hand has guided me today. I woke at morning's dawn afraid to face my problems so I prayed. And one by one each need was met, for Thou hast never failed me yet. Dear God, henceforth my prayer shall be for strong, abiding faith in Thee. Amen.

VIRGINIA SCOTT MAROUS

Dear God, I thank You for my parents...for all their wise and careful instruction. When my feet were small, they lovingly set them upon the right paths. I thank them for all the times they comforted me when I was hurt or afraid and listened to how I felt. As I grew, they showed me to see beauty when I was broken, brought me gladness when I was sad, praised and encouraged me when all seemed lost. Thanks for all their secret prayers for me. They've been my best friends here on earth and if God hadn't chosen them to be my parents…I would have picked them anyway. Amen.

AUTHOR UNKNOWN

7

Read a bedtime poem.

The following poems have been chosen so you can share with your grandchildren good literature that has a moral teaching. As you share with your young ones, be prepared to ponder the thoughts that the writer had in mind. If we want our grandchildren to have good moral character, we must take the time to read and discuss good thoughts which have been written by some of the great minds of our society.

Each poem has its teaching moment. Take time to search for that "kernel of wisdom" which you want your grandchildren to learn. For our grandchildren to take morality seriously, they must have adults who take morality seriously.

Aristotle wrote that good habits formed at youth make all the difference. Bedtime is a wonderful place to teach little by little and precept by precept. Just a few minutes goes a long way in passing wholesome values to the next generation. What a legacy you will leave!

Good and Bad Children
Robert Louis Stevenson

Children, you are very little,
And your bones are very brittle;
If you would grow great and stately,
You must try to walk sedately.

You must still be bright and quiet,
And content with simple diet;
And remain, through all bewild'ring,
Innocent and honest children.

Happy hearts and happy faces,
Happy play in grassy places—
That was how, in ancient ages,
Children grew to kings and sages.

And the unkind and the unruly,
And the sort who eat unduly,
They must never hope for glory—
Theirs is quite a different story!

Cruel children, crying babies,
All grow up as geese and gabies,
Hated, as their age increases,
By their nephews and their nieces.

A Time to Talk
Robert Frost

When a friend calls to me from the road
And slows his horse to a meaning walk,
I don't stand still and look around
On all the hills I haven't hoed,

And shout from where I am, What is it?
No, not as there is a time to talk.
I thrust my hoe in the mellow ground,
Blade-end up and five feet tall,
And plod: I go up to the stone wall
For a friendly visit.

Count That Day Lost
George Eliot

If you sit down at set of sun
And count the acts that you have done,
  And, counting, find
One self-denying deed, one word
That eased the heart of him who heard,
  One glance most kind
That fell like sunshine where it went—Then you
  may count that day well spent.

But if, through all the livelong day,
You've cheered no heart, by yea or nay—
  If, through it all
You've nothing done that you can trace
That brought the sunshine to one face—
  No act most small
That helped some soul and nothing cost—
Then count that day as worse than lost.

8

Share bedtime and the Bible.

Bedtime is such a wonderful time to teach your grand-children about God. Often as adults we wait until there is a problem in our lives, then we try to search out Scripture that will bring us peace in time of trouble.

Take these precious few moments at bedtime to put these promises in your grandchildren's hearts so they are available to memory when trials appear.

You do not have to give a sermon, but let the Scripture take its own course. In some cases you might need to give some insight into what is being conveyed. Indicate that every promise has a condition, and that condition is a responsibility that must be fulfilled if the hearer is to receive that promise.

There are so many promises in Scripture that we are not even aware of. You might catch yourself, the grandparents, saying, "I didn't know that God has given me that promise." Learn to be a doer of the Word, not just a hearer of the Word.

Share with your grandchildren how you have claimed some of these promises and blessings for your own life. These promises and blessings begin to illustrate to your grandchildren how you have let Scripture guide your family's lives. Children love to hear stories.

> Therefore I tell you, whatever you ask for in prayer, believe that you have received it, and it will be yours.
>
> Mark 11:24

> Those who hope in the Lord will renew their strength. They will soar on wings like eagles; they will run and not grow weary, they will walk and not be faint.
>
> Isaiah 40:31

Do not grieve, for the joy of the LORD is your strength.

NEHEMIAH 8:10

Be still, and know that I am God; I will be exalted among the nations, I will be exalted in the earth.

PSALM 46:10

9
Have a "no-shoulds" day.

When the grandchildren come to visit their grandparents for the night or just the waking hours of light, they are usually tired. They have been on a hectic schedule all week with school, sports, music lessons, homework, etc. They would just as soon kick back and get caught up with sleep.

On occasion, plan a "no-shoulds" day. This is a time when nothing is planned: no zoo trips, no Disneyland journey, no movie outings, no special activities. Let them do exactly what they would like to do, and that is usually rest. This is a time to get caught up, to rest, to dream, to read a good book, to listen to good music, with no expectations and no responsibilities. As the kids say, "Just veg out."

How to live a no-shoulds day:

+ Do whatever you want to do: Sleep late, wear your pajamas around the house all day. You do not have to comb your hair or even brush your teeth.

- You can have no meals, or you can have five meals. Have dinner for breakfast and breakfast for dinner. Use only paper products—no dishwashing allowed.

- Watching birds fly and chirp in the yard is permissible. Even tracking a bug crawling over decaying plants is okay.

- Be sure to plan the next "no-shoulds party" before the grandchildren go back home to their demanding routines.

10
Share a thought for the week.

One grandfather states that "his thing" with the older grandchildren is to write each of them (three) a thought for the week—every week! The thought is written out on a 3" x 5" card and hand-selected for each of the three grandchildren. Each thought has a moral or virtue to be discussed. Usually the thought is clear by itself, but occasionally the card must go to Mom and Dad to figure out what Granddad wants the children to know.

These weekly thoughts are a great way to teach without preaching. Below are a few examples of thoughts to send:

> Don't let what you cannot do interfere with what you can do.
>
> JOHN WOODEN

> The harder you work, the luckier you get.
>
> GARY PLAYER

Challenges can be stepping stones or stumbling blocks. It's just a matter of how you view them.

UNKNOWN

If you don't stand for something you'll fall for anything.

UNKNOWN

If you judge people, you have no time to love them.

MOTHER TERESA

I will speak ill of no man, and speak all the good I know of everybody.

BEN FRANKLIN

11
Ring in the season.

Celebrating tradition is not just a matter of proceeding in familiar, well-worn paths trodden by those who came before us. Even as we celebrate the past, we should look forward to the future, planning for memories and establishing new traditions that will shape our celebrations for years to come. After all, the memories of tomorrow are being shaped by the traditions we create today.

Bob and I have had such fun establishing traditions in our family. One of the most meaningful began on our first Christmas together—my very first Christmas as a Christian. Money was tight that year, but we managed to get a tree, and we gave each other ornaments. And we continued to give each other ornaments in the following years. When the children were born, they got ornaments, too. (Years later, when Jenny got married at age 22, we gave Jenny and her husband 22 ornaments to start their own tree.)

And the tradition continues as our family grows. Some years ago I decided not to give ornaments; after 33 years, I thought nobody cared. How wrong I was! Everybody was so disappointed that I went out first thing on December 26 and found just the right ornaments to continue the tradition. And that practice of giving ornaments, begun by Bob and me on our first Christmas together, still warms our hearts when we gather together year after year.

If the grandchildren live away from you, think early and send them their ornaments around the end of November. Over the years, they will look forward to the package that arrives from their grandparents carrying this year's ornaments.

12
Preserve memories of the season's joy.

Traditions have filled our lives with many rare and beautiful treasures over the years, and we have tried to pass those treasures on to our children. We share and celebrate our special ways of doing things, many of which come from the traditions that shaped us.

Our children were already grown and away from home the year I discovered a beautiful Christmas memory book with places to put in photos and write in family memories for every Christmas. "What a great idea!" I exclaimed to Bob. "Too bad we didn't have it 25 years ago." Bob's answer was, "There's nothing wrong with starting now. It's never too late to start a tradition." I am so glad we did, for that book has given us a wonderful record of how our family has grown and changed since we started keeping it.

Each Christmas since that year, we have made a priority of taking a family photo to put into our book. We write down where we celebrated, who was present, what happened, how we felt. It has become a beautiful collection of holiday memories. It shows who gathered with us each Christmas and where we gathered, and it records special holiday events and memories of the past year.

If you are not able to be with your grandchildren for the holidays, send them a photo of your gathering so they can include it in their memory book.

13

Bake memories.

You cannot go wrong when you make cookies with a grandchild. There is so much time to talk, laugh, and share...and the process of making something so delicious is just a bonus. Spend time with a child in your kitchen. The attention to the project somehow opens up the lines of communication. Plan a baking day soon.

Grammy Em's Oatmeal Cookies

Amount: about 4 dozen (5 dozen with coconut)

1. Preheat over to 350°. Grease or spray a cookie sheet.

2. Whisk butter and honey together until well blended and creamy; whisk in egg:

   1 stick (½ cup) soft butter (unsalted preferred)

   ⅔ cup honey

   1 egg

3. Blend dry ingredients in a separate bowl:

   1 cup whole-wheat pastry flour

   1 teaspoon cinnamon

   ½ teaspoon baking soda

   ½ teaspoon salt

   ¼ teaspoon nutmeg

4. With mixing spoon, stir dry ingredients into liquid ingredients just until evenly mixed.

5. Mix in evenly:

   2 cups Quick Quaker Oats, uncooked

   1 cup raisins

   1 cup carob chips or chocolate chips

   1 cup date dices or chopped dates

   1 cup chopped walnuts

   1 cup coconut, unsweetened (optional)— medium or finely shredded

6. Drop by tablespoonfuls onto lightly greased cookie sheet, spacing close together. If dough does not hold together well, press each dropped cookie together a bit with fingertips.

7. Bake at 350° for 10-12 minutes. Cool before removing from cookie sheet.

14
Have a campout...inside.

Plan a fun play date with your grandchildren. Choose an evening when they can stay overnight. Ask them to bring their sleeping bags along and their favorite bedtime stories. When they arrive, have a room all set up with a tent, a snack table, and a circle of space cleared out in the room for the "campfire" time.

You can really have fun with this theme. Add a few well-placed plants, play CDs of nature sounds, turn the lights low, have glow-in-the-dark stars on the ceiling, and you are set.

For activities, you can have the kids roast marshmallows over the stove top with supervision. Sing camp songs and praise songs from church. Pass a flashlight around the circle and have each person share something about himself or herself or read favorite stories. To close the evening circle time, read from Genesis about the creation of nature. Remind them how they, too, were created by the Creator of the earth and sky.

In the morning have a good, camping-worthy breakfast complete with bacon, eggs, and pancakes. Your little guests will be eager to plan the next indoor campout—and so will you!

15

Play Creation.

Another great way to share the Creation story is to dig in and do a little creating of your own.

No-Cook Play Clay

2 teaspoons cooking oil

1 cup salt

1¼ cups water

2 tablespoons cornstarch

3 cups all-purpose flour

Food coloring

In a large bowl, mix cooking oil, salt, and water. Gradually add cornstarch and flour. Knead until smooth. Divide dough into parts and add food coloring. If the dough is too dry, add small amounts of water, and if too sticky, add flour.

Whip up the dough recipe above and prepare for an afternoon of molding, shaping, and creating with your grandchild. As you each take time with your creations, ask these questions to inspire imagination and discussion:

 • Why do you think God formed man and woman?

* God took such care to make us—how do you think He feels about His creation?

* When you make something with this clay, don't you want to protect it? God wants to do the same for us. How does that make you feel?

* What really unique qualities did God give you when He made you?

Father God, raising grandchildren truly is an art. Help me to put in a positive influence on these precious, pliable pieces of clay. I truly want to be a part of molding them into children of God. Amen.

16
Create solid memories.

Let your grandchildren know through work and deeds, that the bond of affection which attaches the two of you to one another can never be broken.

ARTHUR KORNHABER

The moments you spend with your grandchildren create a thread of security in their lives. When you follow through, show up, remember, and keep your word, the foundation of your relationship is solidified.

When you spend a day with your grandchildren, be sure to show them parts of your life. Introduce them to your friends. Take them along when you volunteer. Invite them to your church so they see how you keep your faith strong. Your work and deeds can, indeed, create solid memories and impress on young lives the importance of sharing things that matter.

The following stories are from our family and friends. Since stories often involve time spent with grandmothers, we are sharing a series of stories about the importance of spending special moments and occasions with Grandpa. Regardless of whether it is a grandmother or a grandfather, the story and message is the same: Your time and attention equal fond memories that truly do last a lifetime. Enjoy a sampling of such tales.

PaPa's Adventure Field Trips

I just love to hear PaPa announce that we are going on one of his famous Adventure Field Trips. Over the years I have learned that it's going to be a lot of fun. PaPa always takes us to the best spots to go. We have gone fishing, to the beach, to the big aquarium, football games, to the Lakers basketball game, etc. On and on we go over hill and dell. One of my favorite trips was when we went to Palm Springs for the weekend. Grammy took all the girls to the Spa for a day of spoiling, so PaPa announced that all the boys were going on one of his famous Adventure Field Trips. We all piled in the van and started to drive off into the desert. I don't think PaPa knew where he was going, but he never let on one bit. After about thirty minutes driving, he found an old dirt road off of highway 111 and exited upon this isolated road. Dust was flying behind us and we started to kid him about being lost. He assured us that everything was on schedule—"just sit back and relax," he uttered. In just a few moments, we arrived at this palm tree lined oasis and came upon this art fair. It had many exhibits along with many artisans doing their particular artwork. They invited all of us to join in their activity. We made some beautiful clay pots for Grammy and Mom. I can't wait for PaPa's next Adventure Field Trip.

BRADLEY JOE BARNES

Ice Cream at PaPa's

In the heat of the summer, my PaPa would invite our family over to their home and let us experience making homemade ice cream. Those were the days when there was only the old hand-cranked style. I would go with PaPa to the ice house to purchase the crushed ice and the large-grained kosher salt. Of course, Grandma would have the ingredients already bought and cooking on the stove.

We would come home and pour all the cooked ingredients in a large cylinder, place the lid on top, and position the can just right in the wooden bucket. PaPa would very carefully layer the ice then the salt, more ice and more salt until the ice completely filled the bucket. He took great care to make sure that none of the salt spilled into the ice cream mix.

Then the real fun began: We took turns turning the handle on the freezer. We kept turning for a long, long time. I remember that I got tired turning the handle. When PaPa thought that the ice cream was frozen just right, he would take off the lid to inspect. If it was just right, he would take out the paddle, put the lid back, and pack the freezer with ice to keep the ice cream nice and cold.

PaPa would then start the Bar-B-Que to cook whatever was the specialty of the day. Usually hamburgers, chicken, fish, or meat. Whatever he cooked was delicious, but the best part happened when we had dessert, and we all could eat the homemade ice cream. You know what? All the ice cream was eaten!

BRAD BARNES

PaPa's Pocket

As a small child, I would crawl up on PaPa's lap, and he would hug me with his strong arms. He lived a long way from us, so I didn't have a chance to see him very often.

He lived on a farm with a lot of animals. In the wintertime with snow on the ground, it was too cold to work in the fields, so he had more time for my two brothers and me. His rocking chair was right next to his wood-burning fireplace. It was so cozy on his lap. However, he kind of tricked us to sit on his lap. See, he always had a piece of candy or gum in his shirt pocket. If we sat on his lap, then we could reach into his pocket and get whatever was there. For sure, he knew we always wanted to climb upon his lap and stay for a long time. My PaPa was a very smart man. He knew what would cause us boys to get up on his lap for a very special visit—and a big hug. A lot of times he would take this time to tell us one of his favorite stories. Some were even scary.

KEN BARNES

PaPa's Bag

A few Christmases ago my young grandson, Weston, handcrafted a medium-sized beige canvas bag with a drawstring at the top for his PaPa. On the front of the bag, he printed in a four-year-old's style in bright-colored ink pens the words "PaPa's Bag." He informed me that this bag was to be filled with all kinds of goodies and placed in the backseat of our van. These little morsels of nutrition were to be there when they got into PaPa's car.

Not only do they want PaPa's bag when they are picked up from school or when they come over to spend the night, but grown adults also want PaPa's bag when they are with me.

This bag has been a great conversation piece for me and the grandchildren. On occasion they have informed me, "PaPa you need to fill up your bag with better stuff. It's not too good now." I laugh, but I am off to the market to fill my PaPa's bag with better stuff.

Bob Barnes

The Silly Papa

Soon after our grandson Trey started to walk, play on his own with his toys, and read books, we could see clearly his melancholic/choleric temperament. He instructed us which toy to play with, how and where to stand, or which books to read, etc. When through playing with the toys, for example, he enjoys putting everything back in its proper place as much as he does playing with it.

I noticed when I put something back where it wasn't supposed to go, he would scold me (in a kind way)—"No, Papa, it goes here." That gave me a cue to have some fun with him.

I wanted to provide an element of silliness to his world. So now when I put things away with him, I pretend to put it in a really ridiculous place—like putting a ball in the refrigerator or placing a baseball glove on my head—and he gets the biggest kick out of that. He laughs and laughs until he almost starts coughing at some of my silly antics. Of course, seeing his joyful response only feeds my efforts, and we go on and on.

While reading a book, for example, I will hold it upside down and continue reading like normal, and he will just start with the guffaws. There is really no end to thinking of how to entertain him in this area.

That is my role in his life at this time. He is now 3½, and if I can provide an element of fun, a little different from what my daughter, son-in-law, and my wife offer, then I accept this role with great pride and joy. It is just taking Proverbs 15:30 a step further: "A cheerful look brings joy to the heart."

BOB BROGGER, A SILLY GRANDPA IN CALIFORNIA

17
Speak of God's faithfulness.

Pass along how God has been faithful to your family over the years. These testimonies share how God has provided over the years and also let the grandchildren know about the history of your family. Children love to hear stories. Do not limit your tales to just those of the good times. It is important to share about the hard times, the moments of sadness or burden, and how faith helped a family endure, persevere.

Memory is the great encourager of spirit and life, of correctedness. And rehearsing the past is a sacred practice. It sets the present course. It gives perspective.

STU WEBER

18

Keep the memories alive.

In the future, when your children ask you, "What do these stones mean?" tell them that the flow of the Jordan was cut off before the ark of the covenant of the LORD. When it crossed the Jordan, the waters of the Jordan were cut off. These stones are to be a memorial to the people of Israel forever.

JOSHUA 4:6-7

In Joshua 4:6 we read, "What do these stones mean?" Our country has many monuments erected so that we remember what great events took place in a particular spot. We never want to let future generations forget what great sacrifices were made in order for us to be the person, the family, the nation we are. That is why traditions are so important in life. It is an attempt to pass on to future generations those things of value that have been passed on to us.

Joshua built a monument of stones so that the children of the future would ask, "What do these stones mean?" Then the people could say to them, "Because the waters of the Jordan were cut off before the ark of the covenant of the Lord. When it crossed the Jordan, the waters of the Jordan were cut off. These stones are to be a memorial to the people of Israel forever."

As a father and grandfather, I often wonder what my legacy will be when the Lord calls me home. Will my family remember me as a man who spent his life with hay and stubble, or will they remember that I was a man of God who represented the true virtues of life?

Each day I find myself continuing to make those choices that require commitment to God. I trust that my legacy will reflect the man I have tried to become.

> A man is a success who has lived well, laughed often and loved much; who has gained the respect of intelligent men and the love of children; who has filled his niche and accomplished his task; who leaves the world better than he found it, whether by an improved poppy, a perfect poem or a rescued soul; who never lacked appreciation of earth's beauty or failed to express it; who looked for the best in others and gave the best he had.
>
> ROBERT LOUIS STEVENSON

19
Make an occasion memorable.

Purchase a Bible for each of the grandchildren as they celebrate a certain age. Be sure to have their name embossed on the cover. While many cultures have significant ceremonies and rites of passage traditions, our culture seems to miss that opportunity. So start it up for your own family. And what better way to mark a moment in time than by giving the wisdom of God?

20

Pass along the heritage of hospitality.

Because I first caught the spirit of hospitality from my mother, I am acutely aware of how important it is to pass on this sharing attitude. I am finding a lot of joy in teaching hospitality—not only in the seminars I hold, but also to our granddaughter, Christine (our "princess in training"). Each year since she was three years old, on her July 9 birthday we plan a tea party. This event has become a tradition we both anticipate eagerly—almost more than her birthday party.

The year Christine turned nine, she decided to invite her friend Leah to an "overnighter" at PaPa and Grammy's house. (The tea party would be the next day.) Christine and Leah were excited as their moms dropped them off at our house. They brought their favorite dolls, too, as special tea party guests. As soon as things were settled, we organized and talked about what was to happen. We sat at the break-fast bar off our kitchen, and I had the girls make a list of the coming events.

The girls decided to bake cookies for the party the night before so they would have more time the day of the party to prepare and enjoy the occasion. As soon as our plans were mapped out, we started in on the cookies.

Christine and I have been making cookies together since she was tiny. When we first started, if I was lucky most of the ingredients got into the mixing bowl. Her little hands dumped flour around the bowl and all over the floor. But all that could be cleaned up later; the mess was just part of the fun and teaching. As the years have progressed, Christine is the one who makes the cookies. She can read the recipe and measure ingredients all by herself now.

The girls had elected to have their tea party in the tree house that year. We asked PaPa to carry the child-sized table and chairs from our loft and place them in the tree house. We all decided a white tablecloth would be appropriate for this special event. Next came the centerpiece. The girls scouted the grounds to find just the right flowers and arranged them in a vase along with a candle.

And then it was time to choose the cups. The year before, I had decided it was time to introduce the girls to my 37-year-old china cup and saucer collection. At the time Bob and I were married, my heart's desire was to have china cups and saucers of my own. So over the years, my Bob, along with family and friends, have given me beautiful china cups and saucers for birthdays and other occasions. Each cup in my collection has special stories and memories. When my mother made her home in heaven in 1980, she left me with her collection of eight special ones.

Four years after that, one of the glass shelves in our hutch collapsed, and many of my cups and saucers shattered. Feeling a little shattered myself, I put the broken pieces in a box and decided to put off dealing with them until a later date.

Finally, six years later—and a few weeks before Christine's tea party—I pulled out the box of broken pieces to see if any cups could be recovered and glued back together. Much to my distress, only one cup and saucer could be repaired— the rest were nothing but tiny pieces.

It was then I realized that the material things we treasure here on earth will one day go "poof." Only that which we treasure in our hearts and spirits will be taken with us, so we do well to put our efforts into making memories and sharing love, not jealously guarding our possessions.

That was when I decided it was time for Christine and Leah to enjoy Grammy's collection. As I led the girls over to the hutch, I began to tell them the stories of the cups and saucers. Then I told them that they could choose any one they wanted for the tea party. I wish you could have seen their eyes as they carefully made their choice of the pattern that appealed to them.

As each girl picked up her cup, I told them, "We must be very careful because these cups and saucers are special and delicate. However, should an accident happen and a cup drop and break—well, that would be unfortunate, but it would be okay. You see, Christine and Leah, you are far more precious to Grammy than the cups and saucers."

> A grandchild is a bundle of love wrapped in possibilities. No wonder that every grandbaby is the light of Grandma's eyes.
>
> AUTHOR UNKNOWN

21
Write wisdom on your heart.

Memorize various verses from Proverbs throughout the year, and we guarantee that you will have plenty of opportunities to share them with your grandchildren over the years. While it is nice for them just to think of you as brilliant, you can also take the opportunity to point them back to the Bible's truth and insight.

Listen to your father, who gave you life, and do not despise your mother when she is old.

PROVERBS 23:22

A generous man will prosper; he who refreshes others will himself be refreshed.

PROVERBS 11:25

Where there is no guidance, the people fall, but in abundance of counselors there is victory.

PROVERBS 11:14 NASB

The light of the righteous rejoices, but the lamp of the wicked goes out.

PROVERBS 13:9 NASB

A gracious woman attains honor.

PROVERBS 11:16 NASB

The wise in heart accept commands, but a chattering fool comes to ruin.

PROVERBS 10:8

22
Accept your calling.

I urge you to live a life worthy of the calling you have received. Be completely humble and gentle; be patient, bearing with one another in love.

EPHESIANS 4:1-2

As you accept your age and this time in life, we pray that you will also embrace your calling. Listen to the One who created you. He still speaks to your heart. He knows you better than anyone else. The One who formed you in your mother's womb continues to love you and make plans for you. Do you believe this truth?

Really allow this verse in Ephesians to sink in. Let your every day be worthy of the calling you have received. Your days are of great value. Your life is of tremendous worth. Stand firm in this understanding, and your grandchildren will have memories of your strength and purpose in the Lord. How you live is how you will be remembered.

23

Let love shape every moment.

You will find as you look back upon life that the moments when you have really lived are the moments when you have done things in the spirit of love.

HENRY DRUMMOND

Love casts a different kind of light on a moment shared. When you express your love to your grandchildren, they can feel the warmth of that light. Their gifts will shine when they stand in the rays of your appreciation and attention. Their lives will be brighter because you have loved them completely and unconditionally.

24
Rejoice in this season of life.

Reflect on the following Scripture from Ecclesiastes and take to heart the core of its wisdom: There is a plan, purpose, and orchestrated timing for everything that happens. Rest in this truth. This time of your life is significant, purposeful, and a part of God's plan. The plan continues in the lives of your grandchildren. Let this be a time to love, to give, and to remember.

> To every thing there is a season, and a time to
> every purpose under the heaven:
> A time to be born, and a time to die; a time to
> plant, and a time to pluck up that which is
> planted;
> A time to kill, and a time to heal; a time to
> break down, and a time to build up;
> A time to weep, and a time to laugh; a time to
> mourn, and a time to dance;
> A time to cast away stones, and a time to
> gather stones together; a time to embrace,
> and a time to refrain from embracing;
> A time to get, and a time to lose; a time to
> keep, and a time to cast away;
> A time to rend, and a time to sew; a time to
> keep silence, and a time to speak;
> A time to love, and a time to hate; a time of
> war, and a time of peace.
>
> ECCLESIASTES 3:1-8 KJV

The Legacy
of Faith

Faith

Express your love for your grandchildren with the gift of faith. Extending to them your hope and belief in Christ and His promises will be a lasting legacy—and the most significant. As you read the following ideas, prayers, activities, and devotions, our hope is that you will be inspired to create your own list of ways to share your faith with your grandchildren.

Did you grow up with grandparents who modeled spiritual strength? If so, you understand the importance of living out faith in front of grandchildren. If you did not grow up with this influence, then you understand the void created in a child's life when belief and truth are not modeled by an older generation. Whatever your experience, learn from it. And then give your grandchildren the great gift of great faith. Every effort you make, every conversation you initiate, and every hug you offer to the child in your life will reflect the love of their heavenly Father.

25

Make a commitment.

If you have contact with a grandchild—whether by letters, phone calls, e-mails, or a knock at the door—then you are involved in the raising of that child. Make a commitment today to raise each grandchild in the ways of wisdom, understanding, and knowledge.

Take a vow. Think of each of your grandchildren as you read the vow below. What will this vow mean to your life? Will it change how you interact with your family? Will it change your daily living?

> I promise to share my faith, my life, and my love with my grandchild, even when it involves extra effort...even if it means I will step out of my comfort zone...even though I might have to rearrange my current priorities to do so. I will model all that is important to me so that my grandchild can grow up knowing what a life of faith looks like. Through my actions and my words, I will turn my grandchild's eyes toward Jesus.

Let this vow inspire your daily commitment to sharing the legacy of faith.

26

Rest in the knowledge of the Master Potter.

Behold, like the clay in the potter's hand, so are you in My hand.

JEREMIAH 18:6 NASB

When our son, Brad, was in elementary school, the teacher asked the class to shape clay into something. Molded and shaped with his small hands, this red dinosaur-type thing that Brad proudly brought home is still on our bookshelf today. Now his children are able to view this prized exhibit of their father's artistry.

Later in high school, Brad enrolled in a ceramics class. His first pieces were crooked and misshapen, but as time went on he made some pieces of real art—vases, pots, pitchers, and various other types of pottery. Many pieces of clay he threw on the pottery wheel, however, took a different direction than he had intended. Brad would work and work to reshape the clay, and sometimes he would have to start over, working and working to make it exactly the way he wanted it to be.

With each one of us as grandparents, God has, so to speak, taken a handful of clay to make us exactly who He wants us to be. He is the Master Potter, and we are the vessels in His hands. As He shapes us on the potter's wheel, He works on the inside and the outside. He says, "I am with you. I am the Lord of your life, and I will build within you a strong foundation based upon My Word."

The Master Potter also uses the circumstances of life to shape us. But when a child dies, we lose our job, fire destroys our home, finances dissolve, our marriage falls apart, or our children or grandchildren rebel, the Potter can seem very far away.

We may feel forgotten by God, so we pull away from Him because He "let us down." As time passes, God seems even more silent and distant. It seems like the Potter's work is put on hold. But God said, "I will not fail you or forsake you" (Joshua 1:5 NASB).

When we feel far from God, we need to remember that He did not put us on a shelf. We are the ones who have moved away. He is ready to continue molding us into the people He intends us to be.

In pottery the clay is baked at a very high temperature to set the clay so the vessel won't leak. Sometimes the true beauty of the clay comes out only after the firing. The fires of life can do the same for our faith and our character. When we go through trials as grandparents, we can rest in the knowledge that the Master Potter is at work in our lives.

> Tomorrow may not be—but I have today.
> PEARL YEADON McGINNIS

27
Have a two-fisted faith.

But whoever does not fall down and worship shall immediately be cast into the midst of a furnace of blazing fire.
DANIEL 3:6 NASB

Fortunately for us, who live in the western part of the world, we have not been given this sort of ultimatum. We are free to worship any sort of god we want—either our almighty God, a god of another religion, or a make-believe god of materialism.

In our Scripture reading of Daniel 3, we see that King Nebuchadnezzar wanted his people to bow down before his golden idol or face the consequence of death in a fiery furnace.

As grandparents, we are continually challenged to live a life of faith or to bow down before another false idol. Each day we must decide whom we will serve.

The heroes of this passage are three Israelites: Shadrach, Meshach, and Abednego. They had a choice to make: either to bow down before the king's idol or to be thrown into the hot furnace. To them this was not going to be a big decision. They knew without question that they would not bow down before the false idol. Thus they knew that they were to be cast into a furnace that might consume their bodies. The men in Daniel 3:16-18 give a classic answer to the king:

> O Nebuchadnezzar, we do not need to give you an answer concerning this matter. If it be so, our God whom we serve is able to deliver us from the furnace of blazing fire; and He will deliver us out of your hand, O king. But even if He does not, let it be known to you, O king, that we are not going to serve your gods or worship the golden image that you have set up.

You must read the remainder of Daniel 3 to get the Paul Harvey ending—the rest of the story. These three men had two assurances of faith:

+ God is able.

+ But if not...

These are our two alternatives when difficulties face us. We can be assured that God is able to see us through. But if not, we will not worship any other god. Yes, our two-fisted faith will see us through any and all situations.

28
Walk the talk.

Grandparenting is a marvelous opportunity to keep alive, alert, growing, and giving. When burdens, afflictions, and fears enter our life, we can easily focus on them with all of our energy. God calls us to release those burdens to Him. To be an example of God's love, we must turn over our own life to the Lord, both the problems and the joys.

In your journal, list several of your temporary afflictions. Beside each one write, "This is producing an eternal weight of glory for me." Jot down several struggles you are having in life. Beside each one list several things that God is trying to teach you through that trial.

Father God, thank You again for assuring me that this is not the end, for the end will be an "eternal weight of glory" far beyond all comparison. I trust You for perfecting what is taking place in my life. Amen.

29
Reflect.

Are you fully aware of Christ's presence in Your life? When you believe God is truly connected with your life, it becomes easier to talk with Him, trust Him, and seek His wisdom. As a grandparent, you will draw great strength from your relationship with the Lord. Your grandchildren will be introduced to God's presence and His ways as you share your life and faith. Take time to reflect on the following reading:

> May the wisdom of God instruct me,
> the eye of God watch over me,
> the ear of God hear me, the word of God give
>   me sweet talk,
> the hand of God defend me, the way of God
>   guide me.
> Christ be with me.
> Christ before me.
> Christ in me.
> Christ under me.
> Christ over me.
> Christ on my right hand.
> Christ on my left hand.
> Christ on this side.
> Christ on that side.
> Christ in the head of everyone to whom I speak.
> Christ in the mouth of every person who speaks
>   to me.
> Christ in the eye of every person who looks upon
>   me.
> Christ in the ear of everyone who hears me today.
> Amen.
>
> ST. PATRICK

30
Live for today.

May the God of hope fill you with all joy and peace as you trust in him, so that you may overflow with hope.

ROMANS 15:13

As I have observed my five grandchildren over the years, one thing stands out very vividly: their ability to live and enjoy the moment. They can take the "now" and make it a gift. I am trying to forget about what happened yesterday and what might happen tomorrow and just experience the fullness of today.

In order to capture the present, we need to give less attention to worries, mistakes, what is going wrong, general concerns, things to get done, the past, and the future. *Today I will only think about today. No regrets for the past or fears about the future.* When you do this, all your focus is on the now. You can smile, laugh, pray, think, and enjoy what each moment brings.

Often our anxieties are about situations over which we have no control. I tell the ladies at my seminars that 85 percent of the things we worry about never happen. Why spend all that negative energy on something that probably will never occur?

We are to stop and smell the roses, hear the train whistle, see the puffy clouds in the sky, hear the rain fall, and watch the snow flurries. When we begin to see and experience every minute, we will also begin to see the grandeur of God and His vastness.

31

Share your values.

All things are lawful for me, but not all things are profitable.

1 CORINTHIANS 6:12 NASB

As grandparents, we cannot believe the difference in American values now versus when we were raising our children. While our grandchildren are in our environment, we are responsible for the imagery they receive.

No greater influence impacts our thinking than the media. Unfortunately, the media in America is mostly controlled by secular humanists, so the slant of most print copy, programming, advertising, and news portrays a secular lifestyle.

Secular humanism is the view that man establishes his own moral values apart from the influence of anyone, including God, and the individual determines his own destiny. The individual becomes the master of his own fate.

The problem with such a life view is that it has no absolutes. Everything is relative; there is no eternal reference point. People can make up their own rules as they go. How do we know if sexual promiscuity is immoral or not? Why should we not cheat in business? Why should family life be considered more important than a career?

Ted Koppel, the news anchor for "Nightline," said in a commencement address at Duke University, "We have reconstructed the Tower of Babel and it is a television antenna, a thousand voices producing a daily parody of democracy in which everyone's opinion is afforded equal weight regardless of substance or merit. This means we need to guard our minds more carefully because so many kooky ideas are floating around."

Perhaps the only way to overcome this impact is to reevaluate our sources of entertainment and information. We should be concerned that our subconscious minds might be swayed by unwanted viewing.

As grandparents, we have the opportunity to screen what will be heard and seen. After all, all TV sets have an "on" and "off" button. Don't be apologetic about using it. There are some wonderful alternatives for viewing when the grandchildren come for a visit or a sleepover.

32

Train a child to walk toward blessings.

And if ye walk contrary unto me...will I also walk contrary unto you.

LEVITICUS 26:21,24 KJV

Any responsible parent or grandparent can tell you that you cannot grant to a disobedient child his wishes. If the father does, then he cannot manage his family properly. Sadly, there comes a time when the parent or grandparent must insist that if the child is not obedient to rules of the home or does not listen to the wisdom of the adult, then the child will have to go somewhere else.

God acts toward us as we act to our wayward child. It is not that He does not love us, but He responds with "tough love" because He loves us so much. The child and grandchild is still a member of the family, but he will not receive the many blessings afforded him because he was disobedient to wisdom and truth.

We are amazed when we meet individuals who do not look or act like Christians, but in conversation they share that they attended church when they were younger and accepted Jesus as their personal Savior. Their present lives certainly do not reflect those early childhood decisions, yet they still classify themselves as Christians.

God is longing for them to return to His way. He wants them—and each of us—to share in His great blessings—all of them.

What Is Faith?

Faith is the eye by which we look to Jesus. A dim-sighted eye is still an eye; a weeping eye is still an eye. Faith is the hand with which we lay hold of Jesus. A trembling hand is still a hand. And he is a believer whose heart within him trembles when he touches the hem of the Saviour's garment, that he may be healed. Faith is the tongue by which we taste how good the Lord is. A fever-ish tongue is nevertheless a tongue. And even then we may believe, when we are without the smallest portion of comfort; for our faith is founded not upon feelings, but upon the promises of God. Faith is the foot by which we go to Jesus. A lame foot is still a foot. He who comes slowly, nevertheless comes.

GEORGE MUELLER

33
Create a formula for life.

Seek first His Kingdom and His righteousness, and all these things will be added to you.

MATTHEW 6:33 NASB

We live in a very anxious society. Many of us are more worried about tomorrow than today. We bypass all of today's contentment because of what might happen tomorrow. In Matthew 6:31 we read that the early Christians asked the same basic questions we do: What shall we eat? What shall we drink? What shall we wear?

Jesus tells them in verse 34 (NASB), "So we do not worry about tomorrow; for tomorrow will care for itself. Each day has enough trouble of its own." The formula Jesus gives for establishing the right priorities of life is in today's verse. Emilie and I have used this verse as our mission verse. Each day we claim these two instructions:

Seek *His* kingdom.

Seek *His* righteousness.

Often we are overwhelmed by having too many things to do. Life offers many good choices on how to schedule our time. But we all have only 24 hours a day. How are we to use these hours effectively? When we seek first God's kingdom and His righteousness, we find that our day takes shape. We can say yes, we will do this, or no, we will not do that. When we begin to set priorities, we determine what is important and what is not, and how much time we are willing to give each activity. The Bible gives us guidelines:

- Our personal relationship with Him (Matthew 6:33; Philippians 3:8)

- Our time for home and family (Genesis 2:24; Psalm 127:3; 1 Timothy 3:2-5)

- Our time for work (1 Thessalonians 4:11-12)

- Our time for ministry and community activities (Colossians 3:17)

We cannot do all the things that come our way. Emilie and I have a saying that helps us when we have too many choices: "Say no to the good things; say yes to the best." Do not be afraid to say no. If you have established Matthew 6:33 as one of the key verses in your life, you can very quickly decide whether a particular opportunity will help you.

After learning to say no easily, you can begin to major on the big things of life, like grandparenting, and not get bogged down by minor issues or situations.

34
Show them the way.

Show me your ways, O LORD, teach me your paths; guide me in your truth and teach me, for you are God my Savior, and my hope is in you all day long. Remember, O LORD, your great mercy and love, for they are from of old.

PSALM 25:4-6

Think on Psalm 25:4-6. Once you have memorized it or read over it a few times, then replace the references to God with "Grandma" or "Grandpa." You see…this is what a grandchild is asking of you. Do your ways reflect the Lord? As you lead your grandchildren with your actions and words, which path are you on? Do you give them cause to say they have hope in you?

> Father God, let me be a positive influence upon my children and grandchildren's development into responsible adults who are positive contributors to our society. May my grandchildren know they are loved. May they have hope in me and faith in You, Lord. Amen.

35
Mentor your grandchildren.

Even when I am old and gray, do not forsake me, O God, till I declare your power to the next generation, your might to all who are to come.

PSALM 71:18

As I get older, I think more and more about what comes next. I know that something must follow after this life is over because I cannot grasp the alternatives. I cannot imagine that through all eternity I will never see anyone I love again, that my whole awareness will just be obliterated. I do not believe that we are only bodies passing through.

There is a season of life that challenges our belief in the hereafter. What happens when we die? The psalmist pleads for God not to forsake him until he declares the power of God to the next generation. Wow! What a great prayer! I guess that is why I do what I do. I want to tell everyone, starting with my immediate family and branching out to others, about the power and the might of God.

One of my favorite passages of Scripture gives me a vision of how I can touch the next generation. It is found in Titus 2:3-5: "Likewise, teach the older women to be reverent in the way they live, not to be slanderers or addicted to much wine, but to teach what is good. Then they can train the younger women to love their husbands and children, to be self-controlled and pure." If only we could grasp the vastness of these words. Don't wait until you are old and gray-haired. Begin today!

> Henry Ward Beecher proclaimed, "Children are the hands by which we take hold of heaven." A grandmother, by taking firm hold of her grandchild's hand, creates a little piece of heaven here on earth.

36
Never give up.

That is why we never give up. Though our bodies are dying, our spirits are being renewed every day. For our present troubles are quite small and won't last very long.

Yet they produce for us an immeasurably great glory that will last forever!

2 Corinthians 4:16-17 NLT

If you have financial troubles, setbacks…it's not the end.

If you have been lied to and deceived…it's not the end.

If you have lost your job…it's not the end.

If something has been stolen from you or if you have been robbed of your inheritance…it's not the end.

If you have a child who is ensnared in sin, entangled in a web of wrong relationships, failing according to life's report card, or refusing to communicate with you…it's not the end.

If your mate has walked away, chosen someone else instead of you…it's not the end.

If you have just lost a loved one to death—sudden death, expected or unexpected—it's not the end. Even if your loved one committed suicide…it's not the end.

If you are incarcerated for a crime…it's not the end.

If you are losing your hearing or your sight… it's not the end.

If you are in the depths of depression, if you are battling depression or a chemical imbalance that has thrown all your emotions and even your way of doing things out of kilter…it's not the end.

If you have learned that you have a terminal disease, a crippling disease, a wasting disease...it's not the end.

If you have stepped onto the threshold of death... it's not the end.

I can tell you all this with the utmost of confidence and know that what I am telling you is truth.

It may seem like the end...

You may wish it were the end...

But it is not the end because God is God and the end has not yet come.

FROM A KAY ARTHUR
PRECEPTS MINISTRIES NEWSLETTER*

37
Put faith into action.

Spend quality time with your grandchildren today. Let them see and hear you make godly decisions. Reflect upon this statement: "Our attitude toward our grandchildren reveals our attitude toward God."

When faith is translated into day-to-day behavior, your grandchild will understand the depth of the Christian life. Try to do each of the following this week, and let a child witness your heart for the Lord:

* Used by permission

+ Stop and take time to listen to your grandchildren, eye-to-eye.

+ Be consistent in your training on what is right
and what is wrong.

+ Give your grandchild a beautiful gift today—
TIME!

38
Give a ring and a prayer.

Call your grandchildren today. Ask for them specifically,
so they know you are calling to have a conversation with
them. And in the conversation, share how God has been
faithful to you recently. If you have a lot of grandchildren,
you may want to spread your phone calls over several days.

Not sure what to say? Start off a conversation with some
of these:

"I was just thinking about how good you are at…"

"Something I saw the other day reminded me of
you."

"I think my favorite memory of spending time
with you is…"

"I told a friend of mine that you were a wonderful
grandchild because…"

"The verse I read today meant so much to me,
I wanted to share it with you."

39

Strive to win the race.

And let endurance have its perfect result, so that you
may be perfect and complete, lacking in nothing.

JAMES 1:4 NASB

The Aesop fable about the tortoise and the hare has a lot to teach.

> A hare was one day making fun of a tortoise for being so slow on his feet.
>
> "Wait a bit," said the tortoise. "I'll run a race with you, and I'll wager that I win."
>
> "Oh, well," replied the hare, who was much amused at the idea. "Let's try and see."
>
> It was soon agreed that the fox should set a course for them and be the judge. When the time came both started off together, but the hare was soon so far ahead he thought he might as well have a rest; so down he lay and fell fast asleep. Meanwhile the tortoise kept plodding on and reached the goal. At last the hare woke up with a start and dashed to the finish line, only to find that the tortoise had already won the race.

Too many of us only see the start of the race. So much of life is painted with speed, flash, and sizzle that we can be intimidated. As grandchildren grow, they will encounter a sense of intimidation often. Rely on God's strength and be a person of perseverance. You will introduce your grandchild to a brighter future filled with hope, not fear.

A few years ago our family went to Lake Tahoe to ski during the Christmas break. As we walked on the icy slopes of this beautiful resort, our eyes were full of the best—the best cars, skis, clothes, and beauty. We could not believe our eyes; we had never seen so much sizzle in one place.

So I said to myself, "No way am I going to compete with them." After being coaxed into my group ski lesson, I found that members of the sizzle group were also in my class, and they could not ski any better than I could!

James 1:4 and the fable both teach that perseverance is enduring with patience. In the Bible, perseverance describes Christians who faithfully endure and remain steadfast in the face of opposition, attack, and discouragement. When we persevere with patience, we exhibit our ability to endure with calmness and without complaint. As believers we must daily commit ourselves to godly living.

Commitment and *discipline* are not words that the world is comfortable with. The new millennium wants everything to feel good, but perseverance does not always feel good. It sometimes demands pain and denial of self. That is why trusting and having faith in God's guidance is so important.

Scripture is clear when it teaches we are to persevere:

- In prayer (Ephesians 6:18)
- In obedience (Revelation 14:12)
- In self-control (2 Peter 1:5-7)

Scripture promises us certain blessings if we endure:

- Final deliverance (Matthew 24:13)
- Rewarded faith (Hebrews 11:6)
- Eternal inheritance (Revelation 21:7)

As you live out examples of God's Word, share these Scriptures with your grandchildren. Armed with the power of God's teachings and promises, they will be prepared for the race of life and all that it brings their way.

40
Live well.

Read the quote below and think about what it means to live well. Are you living life as an adventure? Do you pass along this sense of wonder to your grandchild? If not, then why not? Your view of the life God has given you is being passed along to your grandchildren whether you recognize it or not. Be deliberate in the message you are giving them about the value of life. Chances are, God is trying to teach you a few things about life through your grandchildren.

> My message has been very simple. To live well we must have a faith fit to live by, a self fit to live with, and a work fit to live for—something to which we can give ourselves and thus get ourselves off our hands. We cannot tell what may happen to us in the strange medley of life. But we can decide what happens in us…and that is what really counts in the end. How to take the raw stuff of life and make it a thing of worth and beauty—that is the test of living. Life is an adventure of faith, if we are to be victors over it, not victims of it. Faith in the God above us, faith in the little infinite soul within us, faith in life and in our fellow souls—without faith, the plus quality, we cannot really live.
>
> JOSEPH FORT NEWTON

41

Lift them up in prayer.

Dear children, let us not love with words or tongue but with actions and in truth.

1 JOHN 3:18

There is no greater action to express love for our grandchildren than to pray daily for them. In today's world they need all the hedge of protection and direction that they can get. We need also to pray for their parents daily. Prayer is the most powerful parenting tool we can offer.

Finding time to pray as a parent is more challenging, but we as grandparents have much more time. We have plenty of time in our schedule. We just have to make it our priority each day. The next several ways to love your grandchild are ways to pray. The best way to love a child is to lift their lives, dreams, needs, and futures up to God.

Father God, I truly want to be a prayer warrior for my grandchildren. I plead with You for their salvation and their daily walk with You. May they feel and touch Your goodness in their lives. Protect them from any harm. Amen.

42

Pray without ceasing.

You can pray as you live life, be it shopping, taking your daily walk, driving your car on errands, walking the dog, putting on your makeup, brushing your teeth, or even taking a shower.

Allocate a certain part of your daily routine to pray for a particular child. Then as you gather your mail, drive to the store, pray before meals, you will have a chance to pray for each grandchild and your grown children at least once during that day. This practice turns a daily chore into a true labor of love.

Father God, bring to mind each child as they need prayer. You know their every move, their every concern. Lead me to Scriptures that inspire me to pray the right way. Let my heart and spirit be discerning when I listen to my grandkids, so I can truly hear what they are telling me. Ease their worries, anxieties, or burdens. Give them light spirits that trust in You, their heavenly Father. Amen.

43
Pray earnestly.

Pray till prayer makes you forget your own wish, and leave it or merge it into God's will.

FREDRICK W. ROBERTSON

No matter if you live near or far away, you can be faithful in daily prayer for these precious grandchildren and for their parents. As children are raised and look back on what kept them on the straight and narrow, they recall the assurance of a praying parent and/or grandparents.

Prayer is so powerful, many times beyond our own understanding. We know by experience that God listens to and acts upon believers' prayers. Often we do not see immediate changes, but God's clock runs to a different time than our watches.

Scripture gives us many verses to ingrain in our daily prayer lives. One thing is true about children and grandchildren: They both give us plenty of opportunities to pray.

Some wise person told me once, "When children are young, you talk to them about Jesus, and when they get older, you talk to Jesus about them." Such a wise and enlightening remark! However, do not give up praying for your whole family.

As you talk to the Lord, pray that your grandchildren:

+ Fear the Lord and serve Him (Deuteronomy 6:13)

+ Know Christ as Savior (Philippians 3:8-11)

+ Desire the right kind of friends (Proverbs 1:10,15)

+ Will be saved for the right mate (2 Corinthians 6:14)

+ Submit totally to God (James 4:7-8)

+ Honor their parents (Exodus 20:12)

These words, which I am commanding you today, shall be on your heart. You shall teach them diligently to your sons [and daughters] and shall talk of them when you sit in your house.

DEUTERONOMY 6:6-7

44
Put prayer in motion.

If you live apart from your grandchildren, remember to pray as you walk by their pictures on the dresser or as you hang a family photo on the wall. If they are close by, you can pray as you drive to their home or as you drive by their school.

Pray about their:

+ safety

+ physical health

+ friends

+ closeness with God

+ relationship with family

+ education and mental health

+ future

45
Record your prayers.

In your prayer closet or special nook in the house, write down in your journal what you want to pray for each of the grandchildren. Do not trust your memory—write it down. If you created a prayer notebook, look at the photos of each of your grandchildren. That way you can look into their eyes and faces as you pray.

Think about these questions as you decide what to pray:

+ When you saw the child last, what was his or her mood and attitude?

+ Are there upcoming events that might cause excitement or worry for the child?

+ What are three things this child has done to make you smile?

+ What is your wish for this child in the upcoming year?

46

Call upon the prayers of other people.

Ask your friends and Bible study or Sunday school group members to pray for your grandchildren. The more the merrier! Let other grandparents know that you will pray for their grandchildren if they will pray for yours.

If you are not yet networked with other grandparents, look into community groups or church groups that are already gathering. If you do not find anything, start something. The rewards of praying for one another's families is such a blessing. Soon you will feel the awesome sense of belonging to God's worldwide, extended family.

47

Reflect on the legacies you have been given.

As a young boy of nine, I (Bob) experienced one of my favorite bonding moments with my grandfather on my father's side. He was a robust cotton farmer with hands of steel and a heart for God. Every Sunday morning while we would visit our "Papa," he would take us to Anderson Chapel Methodist Church on the outskirts of Anson, Texas. As we began to sing, Papa's rough voice would utter these words: "I come to the garden alone, while the dew is still on the roses, and the voice I hear falling on my ear, the Son of God discloses. And He walks with me, and He talks with me, and He tells me I am His own; and the joy we share as we tarry there, none other has ever known."

I will always remember this great scene. It made such an impression on a young boy's heart that it has stayed with me for more than six decades.

This great gospel song, "In the Garden," was written by C. Austin Miles in 1912 after he read the Scripture verse where Mary Magdalene came to the garden and then told the disciples that she had seen the Lord (John 20:18).

Quite often as I work in my own garden in the cool of the morning before the noonday heat arrives, I catch myself singing the words to this beautiful hymn. The words and melody are so soothing to my spirit. I know without a doubt that God walks with me, and He talks with me, and He tells me I am His own.

I am not even sure that Papa ever knew of the legacy he left with me.

48
Teach key Scripture passages.

Even young children can begin to memorize specific verses and ideas from the following four treasured Scripture passages. Post these in your home. Write them out and send them to your grandkids. Reference these cornerstone verses in your conversations so they equate God's Word with lessons for living.

If your grandkids are reading, have them look up various translations for these verses so they can see the subtle differences of expression. A certain word change might spark a strong connection in their minds and hearts. These are in the King James Version.

The Twenty-third Psalm

The LORD is my shepherd; I shall not want. He maketh me to lie down in green pastures: he leadeth me beside the still waters. He restoreth my soul: he leadeth me in the paths of righteousness for his name's sake. Yea, though I walk through the valley of the shadow of death, I will fear no evil: for thou art with me; thy rod and thy staff they comfort me. Thou preparest a table before me in the presence of mine enemies: thou anointest my head with oil, my cup runneth over. Surely goodness and mercy shall follow me all the days of my life: and I will dwell in the house of the LORD for ever.

The Ten Commandments

Share the Ten Commandments with your grandchildren by reading Exodus 20:2-17. Focus on those which are the most age-appropriate for discussion.

1. I am the LORD thy God....Thou shalt have no other gods before me.

2. Thou shalt not make unto thee any graven image.

3. Thou shalt not take the name of the LORD thy God in vain.

4. Remember the sabbath day, to keep it holy.

5. Honour thy father and thy mother.

6. Thou shalt not kill.

7. Thou shalt not commit adultery.

8. Thou shalt not steal.

9. Thou shalt not bear false witness against thy neighbor.

10. Thou shalt not covet.

The Lord's Prayer—Matthew 6:9-13

Our Father which art in heaven, Hallowed be thy name. Thy kingdom come. Thy will be done in earth, as it is in heaven. Give us this day our daily bread. And forgive us our debts, as we forgive our debtors. And lead us not into temptation, but deliver us from evil: For thine is the kingdom, and the power, and the glory, for ever. Amen.

The Beatitudes of Christ—Matthew 5:3-10

Blessed are the poor in spirit: for theirs is the kingdom of heaven.

Blessed are they that mourn: for they shall be comforted.

Blessed are the meek: for they shall inherit the earth.

Blessed are they which do hunger and thirst after righteousness: for they shall be filled.

Blessed are the merciful: for they shall obtain mercy.

Blessed are the pure in heart: for they shall see God.

Blessed are the peacemakers: for they shall be called the children of God.

Blessed are they which are persecuted for righteousness' sake: for theirs is the kingdom of heaven.

49
Evangelize your grandchildren.

One of the great privileges of being a grandparent is to teach our grandchildren about our faith in Jesus. We have a wonderful opportunity of living our faith in front of these precious children. They will pick up very quickly that Jesus means a lot to us. Our lives can show our thankfulness when we give blessings at mealtime, by our language of appreciation for all that God does for us in good times as well as difficult times, by awareness that we start each day with a "quiet time" with our Lord, and when they hear constantly how the Bible is PaPa and Grammy's source of guidance. Bedtime is a special time to quiet our hearts and bodies for a good night's sleep. We show a good video, listen to good music, read a good story, and end our time with a good-night prayer.

All believers have the assignment to live a godly life before their children and grandchildren, tell them about the Lord, and love them (Deuteronomy 6:7). Nowhere in Scripture is there the suggestion that children are incapable of responding to God or of engaging in song, worship, prayer, and thanksgiving. Jesus shared that children are not required to become adults in order to come to the Father, but that we as adults should become as little children (Matthew 18:3-4).

50
Read your Bible and reflect on your grandkids.

In your daily reading of Scripture, jot down the examples of godly character you run across in the various stories. Pray for your own grandchildren to develop these same qualities: Daniel's courage, Esther's faithfulness, Paul's boldness, etc.

In your prayer journal, list the godly characteristics you currently see in each grandchild. Now list those characteristics you pray for them to embrace. Beside each of these, write down how you can encourage the child in that particular area of life. If a grandchild needs courage, perhaps you will want to encourage that child more often. Or maybe you will make the decision to invite that child on some kind of adventure where he can stretch his wings and step out in faith.

There are so many ways that reading Scripture can tie back into how you treat and train your grandchildren. Be a willing student of the Bible, and you will be excelling in the Grandparenting 101 class.

51
Have your home reflect God.

The special touches in your home can create a secure haven for your grandchildren. Place photos of the kids and pieces of their artwork in every room of your home. Be sure to place a few at eye level for the little ones. They will feel at home and will realize how much you include them in your daily life.

A child might only have a few truly safe, loving places during his or her childhood. Do everything you can to surround your grandchildren with images that reflect the importance of faith, family, and children.

> Father God, thank You so much for giving me the desire to create a home for our family. The children and grandchildren always love to come back home. I am truly receiving all of Your blessings for being a homemaker. Amen.

The Legacy
of Life

Life

But the fruit of the Spirit is love, joy, peace, patience, kindness, goodness, faithfulness, gentleness and self-control. Against such things there is no law. Those who belong to Christ Jesus have crucified the sinful nature with its passions and desires. Since we live by the Spirit, let us keep in step with the Spirit.

GALATIANS 5:22-25

As we live out our lives and persevere daily against all the trials and temptations, we are rewarded by the Lord with the fruit of His Spirit for all eternity. Look at the list again…the list of all the things you desire to be, hope to embrace, and love to celebrate:

Love	Goodness
Joy	Faithfulness
Peace	Gentleness
Patience	Self-control
Kindness	

These are the rewards and legacies of a life lived fully in Christ. Share your hunger for the fruit of His Spirit, and your grandchildren will also desire such sustenance.

Find ways to share each of these characteristics of the Christian life. When you turn to your prayer journal, take time to pray specifically about ways to show love, joy, peace, patience, kindness, goodness, faithfulness, gentleness, and self-control.

52

Teach by example.

I exhort you, therefore, be imitators of me.

1 CORINTHIANS 4:16 NASB

One night when a grandfather was praying with his grandson, the boy asked a very penetrating question.

"Granddad, have I ever met a Christian?"

The grandfather was taken aback, realizing that his grandson had not caught what he was attempting to teach the lad.

Are you living for Christ in a way that you are modeling Christ to your children and grandchildren?

In bygone days, a father who was a skilled tradesman would take on his son as an apprentice. This required many years of training so the apprentice could qualify as a journeyman. This was teaching by example. There are very few trades that are taught like that anymore; vocations have become far too complex.

However, in the family setting, children still learn by example. They learn by seeing Mom, Dad, and grandparents in action. They see their adults' values and ethics put into practice.

Your "little apprentices" are watching everything you do in the car, at a ball game, in church, around the meal table— everywhere! These are great opportunities to teach your grandchildren the important values of life. Children's eyes are always open to example.

53
Build a balanced home.

Unless the LORD builds the house, they labor in vain who build it; unless the LORD guards the city, the watchman keeps awake in vain.

PSALM 127:1 NASB

As grandparents, we sometimes wonder if we actually have a home—or is it merely a stopover place to eat, do laundry, hang around, and sleep? Is it just a place to repair things, mow the lawn, paint, wallpaper, and install new carpet? A true home is much more than all that. It is a place of people living, growing, laughing, crying, learning, and creating together.

A small child, after watching his house burn down, was quoted as saying, "We still have a home. We just don't have a house to put it in." How perceptive!

We do not have to be perfect—just forgiven. We can grow, we can make mistakes, we can shout for joy, we can cry, we can agree, and we can disagree. Home is a place where happy experiences occur. It is a place sheltered from the problems of the world, a place of love, acceptance, and security.

When we read the newspaper, we are confronted with all the tragedies around us, and we realize that the world outside our front door is falling apart. But within our four walls, we can offer a place of peace.

What can we do to have a home like God intended? As with everything in life, when something is broken, we go back to the instruction book—and life's manual is the Bible. The home is God's idea. He designed the home to be the foundation of society—a place to meet the mental, spiritual, physical, and emotional needs of people.

The members of a family must work together to make their house a true home—not just a place where they live. It is impossible to do this by our own efforts; we are not strong enough to accomplish the task. We must turn our hearts, souls, and lives to God's Son, Jesus Christ. He is our source of strength.

54
Pray about the future.

In your prayer journal, jot down aspects of the future and write down specifics related to each child. Include what might be their concerns or dreams regarding:

+ family
+ college or training
+ marriage
+ raising kids of their own
+ their future calling
+ their vocation and occupation

Father God, we think we only live for today, but Scripture tells us to look to the future and eternity. The world wants us to conform to the pressures of the here and now and focus on the temporal. Help me to take time to develop a future orientation for myself and my family. What You have done for us in the past gives us hope for the future. Amen.

55

Use the "how" word.

How blessed is the man who finds wisdom, and the man who gains understanding.

PROVERBS 3:13 NASB

This little word *how* is a marvelous word that is used throughout Scripture. As a grandparent, one can certainly use this word time and again. However, when it is used, I often add another word to it to express my reflection upon being a grandparent: *how blessed, how majestic, how lovely, how good, how happy, how sweet, how precious, how delightful.* The list goes on and on. We use these add-on words to describe our love for these young lives that God has given us.

Emilie and I often say to each other, "If we would have known that grandchildren would be so much fun, we would have had them first." Tongue-in-cheek humor, but true. We are able to give our grandchildren what we were not always able to give to our own children: TIME.

Throughout Scripture we find the writers using *how* to describe some aspect of God's influence to mankind. For example:

* How blessed is the man who does not walk in the counsel of the wicked(Psalm 1:1 NASB).

* How delightful is a timely word (Proverbs 15:23 NASB).

* How happy is the man whom God reproves (Job 5:17 NASB).

* How blessed is the man who finds wisdom (Proverbs 3:13 NASB).

- How precious is [His] lovingkindness (Psalm 36:7 NASB).

- How devoutly and uprightly and blamelessly [Paul] behaved (1 Thessalonians 2:10 NASB).

- How great a love the Father has bestowed on us, that we would be called children of God (1 John 3:1 NASB).

- How majestic is [His] name in all the earth (Psalm 8:1,9 NASB).

- How lovely are [His] dwelling places (Psalm 84:1 NASB).

- How awesome are [His] works (Psalm 66:3 NASB).

- How good and how pleasant it is for brothers to dwell together in unity (Psalm 133:1 NASB).

- How sweet are [His] words...sweeter than honey (Psalm 119:103 NASB).

- How unsearchable are His judgments (Romans 11:33 NASB).

So you can see that this three-letter word is very powerful in Scripture. May we realize that it has real meaning for us as grandparents. It hopefully helps to describe our grandchildren. If not, make it a part of your teaching time when they are in your presence.

56
Get on your knees.

This week you have the opportunity to get on the floor and build block towers. This is the season when you are invited to read, to play, to imagine, to dream! Your lap is the "favorite-est place to be." Your smile is more valuable than money. Your words mean more than those on the television, in a magazine, or in a classroom. Savor the moments of this season that will never come around again.

We tend to believe that life will get better, when really it just gets different. If the grass looks greener on the other side of your fence, it may be because you are not investing your time and energy in your own grass. Live in the present.

And while you are on your knees playing, don't forget the praying.

57
Forget lectures...share lessons.

You shall teach them diligently to your sons [grandchildren] and shall talk of them when you sit in your house and when you walk by the way and when you lie down and when you rise up.

DEUTERONOMY 6:7 NASB

Moses directed the Israeli nation to do everything possible to remember the commands (the sum and substance of the Law) and to incorporate them into everyday life. Part of this included the spiritual education of the children. In

Hebrew the word for "parent" is *teacher*. As grandparents, we become grand teachers. Just because we are not the parent, we still have responsibilities to continue teaching when we are with our grandchildren.

Spiritual teaching in Bible times would take place daily through the study of God's Word, the recitation of the Law, and the examples the parents and grandparents exhibited in their lives. The instruction was more than just the reading and memorization of the Law. It included the demonstration of a godly lifestyle woven into everyday living.

We grandparents have to be creative in the ways we teach. We need to be alert to life and the events that are happening around us. Use the news to point out examples of good and evil. The seasonal holidays are great opportunities to evaluate the origins of each celebration. Anniversaries, birthdays, weddings, funerals, and new births are perfect times to instruct your children in God's laws. Strolling on the beach, hiking, sleeping out under the stars, cooking together, or working on a car can be treasured moments to teach truths.

As grandparents, we are always teaching—which is different than lecturing. Remain open to questions. Watch your nonverbal language when shocking comments come forth. Pray for wisdom, guidance, and patience before and during your times with your grandchildren.

> The role of a teacher is one of the most important for any grandparent.
>
> ARTHUR KORNHABER

58

Share whatever is good.

Go to the Christian bookstore and select some wholesome videos or DVDs for when the grandchildren come to visit. Meditate on the following Scripture during your time of prayer today:

> *Finally, brothers, whatever is true, whatever is noble, whatever is right, whatever is pure, whatever is lovely, whatever is admirable—if anything is excellent or praiseworthy—think about such things. Whatever you have learned or received or heard from me, or seen in me—put it into practice. And the God of peace will be with you.*
>
> PHILIPPIANS 4:8-9

59

Take the inheritance challenge.

> *A good man leaves an inheritance for his children's children.*
>
> PROVERBS 13:22 NASB

Not too many years ago we were challenged to have a trust and will drawn up by our family attorney who specializes in these areas. We knew that because of the way our taxes are structured, if something would happen to one of us, our estate would be locked up in a mountain of laws and regulations.

As we were deciding on how our estate would be divided, this particular verse of Scripture challenged us to leave part of our worldly possessions to our five grandchildren. Not only were they listed as beneficiaries, but we set up a California Gift to Minors trust fund for each of them with our stockbroker. Each birthday and each Christmas we contribute so much money into each account. On their eighteenth birthday, it becomes theirs to be used for their college education.

In the process, they are learning about mutual funds and the stock market. What a delight to see them take an interest in financial matters.

60
Run the race of life as a victor.

However, I consider my life worth nothing to me, if only I may finish the race and complete the task the Lord Jesus has given me—the task of testifying to the gospel of God's grace.

ACTS 20:24

Most of us as grandparents have already run most of the race of life. In some cases, we are winners. Some of us did not finish the race as we would have liked. Some of us are still running the race. No matter where we are in life's race, we now have the opportunity to help our grandchildren run the race.

We are challenged by our age and position in life to get them off to a running start. Life will be more difficult for those coming behind us than during our growing-up years. The culture and technology have exploded so fast that many times we are not quite sure what is happening. One legacy that we can leave with our grandchildren is that we helped them with this race called life. Each of us has a different calling on how we will do this, but each of us can map out how we will do it. Rich or poor, we can offer much to these youngsters. Just be available with your various resources.

> The very fact that you don't look or act or feel like the grandparents of even a generation ago does not mean that you are less, but that you are more—in effect, an evolved form of grandparents, primed to do a bigger and more challenging job than any group before you.
>
> ARTHUR KORNHABER

61
Never fear.

Children are the most wholesome part of the race, the sweetest, for they are the freshest from the hand of God. Whimsical, ingenious, mischievous, they fill the world with joy and good humor. We adults live a life of apprehension as to what they will think of us; a life of defense against their terrifying energy; a life of hard work to live up to their great expectations. We put them to bed with a sense of relief—and greet them in the morning with delight and anticipation. We envy them the freshness of adventure and the discovery of life. In all these ways, children add to the wonder of being alive. In all these ways, they help to keep us young.

HERBERT HOOVER

Haven't we all been a bit scared of a child? As Herbert Hoover pinpoints, "their terrifying energy" can send us running to the other room, unsure of how to be in the presence of such life. Or it can be tempting to place our hands over our ears to muffle the cries or hollers or shrill laughter of an expressive child.

But to truly love children, we must not base our relationship on fear of them. They sense it. They shy away from adults who tense up in their presence. And sadly, they may interpret our hesitation and reservation as a sign of dislike or disapproval.

Do not send confusing messages to those you cherish. Step into their world of wonder and boisterous communication. Let yourself abandon the orderly life you have created...and step into the chaos. You might reconnect with that "whimsical, ingenious, mischievous" part of you and find that you like yourself all the more.

62
Know the bent of your grandchild.

Train a child in the way he should go, and when he is old he will not turn from it.

PROVERBS 22:6

As I think about our children, Brad and Jenny, and look into the various shades of color in the eyes of our grandchildren—Christine, Chad, Bevan, Bradley Joe II, and Weston—I see seven unique people. How am I ever going to understand the uniqueness of each of these children?

I know that I have to attempt to understand each of them if I am going to have an impact upon molding a healthy, godly character in their lives. At the heart of each child is a cry: "Please take time to know me. I am different from anyone else. My sensitivity, my likes, dislikes, tenderness of heart are different from my brothers and sisters."

In raising our own children, we saw so many differences between Jenny and Brad. Even as adults they are still different. I, in God's wisdom, had to realize that my approach to motivating them had to be styled differently for each of them. Children want to be trained in a personal and tailor-made way.

In our verse for today, we first see the word *train*. In the Hebrew, this word originally referred to the palate (the roof of the mouth) and to the gums. In Bible times, the midwife would stick her fingers into a sweet substance and place her fingers into the new child's mouth, creating a sucking desire in the child. The child would then be delicately given to the mother, whereby the child would start nursing. This was the earliest form of "training." The child mentioned in this text can fall between a newborn and a person who is of marrying age.

The second part of this verse is, "when he is old he will not turn from it." At first I thought this meant an older person who had become wayward, yet finally returned to the Lord. Little did I know that this word *old* meant "bearded" or "chin." Solomon is talking about a young man who begins to grow a beard when he approaches maturity. For some it might be in junior high school, and for others it might be in college. The concept is that we as parents are charged to continue training our children as long as they are under our care.

Note that we are to train a child in *his* way—not our way, our plan, our idea. It is important to see that the verse is not a guarantee to parents that raising a child in God's way means he will return back again when he is old. I honestly do not believe this is the proper principle for us as parents to obtain from this verse. When we train our children according to "his way"—the child's way—we approach each child differently. We do not compare them one to another. Each child is uniquely made.

When I became a student of my two children, I began to design different approaches for each child. Jenny was not Brad, and Brad certainly was not Jenny. Each child has his or her own bent that is already established when God places that child in our family. God has given you unique children and grandchildren. Get to know each one.

63
Recognize the importance of a name.

Think about how the name of your grandchild brings you joy. Think about how his or her name is part of a flowing, growing list of people who make up your family's legacy. If you have the information available, write out the list of names in the generations before your grandchild. Give your grandchildren the gift of belonging...the gift of being a special person who links the past with the present and the future. Present your grandchild with the list at a special time, such as a milestone birthday or when he or she is baptized.

64

Be a grandparent...the kids already have friends.

I will walk within my house in the integrity of my heart.

PSALM 101:2 NASB

In George Washington's day, two candidates applied for a certain office. One was a warm friend and lifelong associate of Washington; the other, decidedly hostile to the politics of Washington, arrayed himself in the ranks of the opposition. It was supposed that Washington would decide for his friend; but, to the surprise of all, the other person was appointed to office.

Upon being remonstrated, Washington replied,

> My friend I receive with a cordial welcome to my house and welcome to my heart; but, with all his good qualities, he is not a man of business. His opponent is, with all his hostility to me, a man of business. My private feelings have nothing to do in this case: I am not George Washington, but president of the United States. As George Washington, I would do this man any kindness in my power; but, as president, I can do nothing.

What a great example of integrity! As grandparents, we must step back and objectively evaluate positions. As I observe changes in our social structure, I see that too many parents and grandparents consider their children friends. When this happens, they lose a key parental role by making decisions based on friendship rather than good parenting.

Grandparents are to be friendly and just, but above all they must be people of integrity.

65
Trust the refiner.

*I will bring that group through the fire and make them
pure, just as gold and silver are refined and purified
by fire. They will call on my name, and I will answer
them.*

ZECHARIAH 13:9 NLT

In the process of refining our lives, God allows and uses
our suffering. My friends Glen and Marilyn Heavilin, for
instance, know the kind of suffering Job knew. They have
lost three sons—one in crib death, one twin by pneumonia,
and the second twin by a teenage drunk driver. Glen and
Marilyn were tested, but they have come through the
Refiner's fire. Today they use their experiences to glorify
the name of the Lord.

Marilyn has written *Roses in December,* which is the story
of how they lost their sons. She has had the opportunity
to speak all over the country in high school auditoriums
filled with teenagers. There she shares her story and talks
about life and death, chemical dependency, and God.

They have come forth as gold fired in the heat of life,
and they are able to shine for Him. Their pain will never
be gone, but they still minister. They have been very active
in "Compassionate Friends," a support group for families
who have experienced the death of children. God knew the
path the Heavilins would take when they faced their tragic
losses, and He has been there as their faith in Him has been
purified.

Every one of us has experienced some kind of tragedy.
It is not the specifics of the event that matter as much as

how we handle it. Whatever loss you are dealing with and however you are being tested, you can be sure that other people have been tested that way, too. So do not go through the testing alone. Trust in God, and find someone you can trust who will bear the burden with you. You, too, can and will come forth as gold.

Remember that Jesus knows your pain, and He is always with you to help you get through the tough times in life. Trust Him now. It is all part of the "coming forth as gold" that Job talks about:

> But he knows the way that I take; when he has tested
>   me, I will come forth as gold.
> My feet have closely followed his steps;
> I have kept to his way without turning aside.
> I have not departed from the commands of his lips;
> I have treasured the words of his mouth more than
>   my daily bread.
>
> Job 23:10-12

66
Surround yourself with inspiring words.

If you feed your spirit with God's Word and inspirational ideas, your attitude will reflect hope and light. Grandchildren want a grandparent who is fun and pleasant. Don't become some cranky, distant adult in a child's life. You are God's child. Let that promise be the spring in your step, the spirit in your laugh, and the sweet truth you share with a grandchild.

Here are some encouraging words *about* life to *feed* your life!

> The quality of a person's life is in direct proportion to their commitment to excellence, regardless of their chosen field of endeavor.
>
> VINCE LOMBARDI

> Some goals are so worthy, it's glorious even to fail.
>
> AUTHOR UNKNOWN

> I am only one; but still I am one. I cannot do everything, but still I can do something; I will not refuse to do the something I can do.
>
> HELEN KELLER

> Hold yourself responsible for the higher standard than anyone else expects of you. Never excuse yourself.
>
> HENRY WARD BEECHER

> Courage is resistance to fear, mastery of fear, not absence of fear.
>
> MARK TWAIN

> No legacy is so rich as honesty.
>
> WILLIAM SHAKESPEARE

> Man's mind once stretched by a new idea, never regains its original dimension.
>
> OLIVER WENDELL HOLMES

> You see things that are and say, "Why?" But I dream things that never were and say, "Why not?"
>
> GEORGE BERNARD SHAW

67
Keep climbing the mountain.

My help is from Jehovah who made the mountains! And the heavens too!

PSALM 121:2 TLB

As I (Emilie) have walked through my cancer treatment these last seven years, I have often wondered if I am going to make it. Yes, my support group has encouraged me. Hundreds and hundreds of prayer partners have assured me by cards and letters that I am going to make it. My mind, however, is sometimes plagued with negative thoughts about my future. Satan so wants to defeat me by making me lose hope for recovery. Yet my faith remains victorious, and my daily walk with God helps me climb the many mountains put before me.

Bill Martin, Jr. tells a story of how a young Indian boy was able to overcome his fear of failure:

> "Grandfather, will I ever be strong like you?" the little boy asked.
>
> His grandfather reassured him, "You're growing stronger every day."
>
> "How strong must I be, Grandfather?" the boy asked.
>
> "You must be so strong that you will not speak with anger even when your heart is filled with anger.... You must be so strong that you will listen to what others are saying even when your own thoughts are begging for expression.... You must be so strong that you will always stop to remember what happened yesterday and foresee what

will happen tomorrow so that you will know what to do today."

"Then will I be strong enough to cross over the dark mountains?" the boy asked.

The wise grandfather answered, "You already have crossed some of the dark mountains, my grandson. But these mountains of sorrow have no beginning and no ending. They are all around us. We can only know that we are crossing them when we want to be weak but choose to be strong."

When you are called to cross the dark mountains surrounding you, be brave even when you feel weak. Lift your face skyward and pray that God will give you strength far beyond your expectation.

68
Know you are being watched.

So take a new grip with your tired hands, stand firm on your shaky legs, and mark out a straight, smooth path for your feet so that those who follow you, though weak and lame, will not fall and hurt themselves, but become strong.

HEBREWS 12:12-13 TLB

Illness often changes our appearance. I guess being bald is common to those patients who have had heavy dosages of chemotherapy. As my hair started to fall out in the shower and on my pillowcase, I wondered, *How can I turn this lemon into lemonade?* I decided to have a "haircut party" with my family.

As we gathered that day on the patio, my son, Brad, brought his razor that he uses on the boys for their summer butch haircuts, and he gave me a buzz cut. The children and grandchildren were all gathered around to observe and to take a few historic pictures. I looked so cute that all the men and boys decided they wanted a buzz cut so they could be just like Grammy. However, our daughter, Jenny, said, "Mom, I love you a whole lot, but I'm not going to get a crew cut." I did not blame her a bit.

This was one of my fond memories of a bad occasion. Everyone was watching to see how I would react. My reaction set the tone for them. I modeled joy for them in a difficult situation. And they were watching me! I helped ease their fear and concern, and this ceremony gave us a way to come together as a family, acknowledge the journey I was on, and unite in love and happiness.

69
Thank God for the cycle of life.

How far you go in life depends on your being tender with the young, compassionate with the aged, sympathetic with the striving, and tolerant of the weak and the strong. Because some day in life you will have been all of these.

GEORGE WASHINGTON CARVER

It can be easy to long for a previous stage of life or lament, "If only I knew then what I know now." You may have friends who spend their moments caught up in this kind of thinking. Maybe it is you. Instead of giving your time over to wasted moments, celebrate where you are in the cycle of life.

You are lucky. You have "been there, done that," as the popular saying goes. Therefore, you are in a very special position to share tenderness, wisdom, and life lessons with your grandchildren. Do not regret your standing as an older person. Embrace it and thank God for bringing you to this place of life.

> Father God, thank You for where I am today in my life. You have brought me far along this path. I am blessed in so many ways. Let me turn over those areas of my life that are stumbling blocks...that weigh me down with regret or woe. I want to live light! And as I do, I want to reflect Your light. Amen.

70
Earn their respect.

Grandchildren are the crown of old men, and the glory of sons is their fathers.

PROVERBS 17:6 NASB

What a great thrill it is to hear my grandchildren say with honor, "This is my dad." One of the Ten Commandments says that we are to honor our mothers and fathers (Exodus 20:12). We live in a time when many children and fathers do not honor each other. I cannot think of a more wasted life than to have children and grandchildren who do not honor their father and grandfathers. If this were true for me, I would rightly think that somewhere along the way I made some bad choices. Oh yes, there are some children who show irreverence to parents unjustifiably. But children mainly reflect back to us how we have behaved toward them.

A good test of whether you are a father or a grandfather who is respected by his children is to ask yourself, "Do I want my grandson or granddaughter to grow up and be like me?"

One way we as Christians need to be a spiritual witness to the world is through the ways our families are different— that we reflect respect and honor for other people.

> Gentleness is love in society....It is that cordiality of aspect and that soul of speech, which assure that kind and earnest hearts may still be met with here below. It is that quiet influence, which, like the scented flame of an alabaster lamp, fills many a home with light and warmth and fragrance alto-gether. It is the carpet, soft and deep, which, whilst it diffuses a look of ample comfort, deadens many a creaking sound. It is the curtain, which from many a beloved form wards off at once the summer's glow and the winter's wind. It is the pillow on which sickness lays its head and forgets half its misery, and to which death comes in a balmier dream. It is considerateness. It is ten-derness of feeling. It is warmth of affection. It is promptitude of sympathy. It is love in all its depths and all its delicacy. It is every thing included in that matchless grace, the gentleness of Christ.
>
> Dr. J. Hamilton

71

Appreciate your purpose and plan.

I will give thanks to You, for I am fearfully and wonderfully made.

PSALM 139:14 NASB

Irene became a single working parent after her husband died. To survive, she opened a small dress shop and lived in the back with her young daughter in a small three-room apartment. Home and career were all mixed together. She not only sold clothing, but she also worked late into the night doing alterations. Book work for her little struggling business had to be done after hours when she was dog-tired.

But despite the hard times, there was a sense of loveliness about her. There were always fresh flowers; simple, creative meals; friends to love and cherish; and each day she lived, the nurturing of the young daughter she loved so dearly.

Above all, my mama, Irene, was a brave woman. I am so thankful that she stood up to my father and said she would have no more abortions. She had already had two previous ones to please him. Because of her bravery, I was able to be born and to fulfill the life that God had for me.

Little did I know when I was conceived in my Jewish mother's womb that many years later I would accept Jesus as my Messiah and my personal Savior. Little did my family realize that my name was long ago written in His book.

Mama didn't have the kind of life I have loved and enjoyed with Bob and our precious children—and now grandchildren. It was a hard life. But through all the abuse, the alcohol-related problems with my father, the financial difficulties and anger in our home, Mama remained a soft, gentle-spirited woman who accepted Jesus as her Messiah and changed her address from earth to heaven when she died at 78 years of age.

God planned for me a long time ago. He has had a plan for my life even before I was born—before my mother had even thought to name me Emilie Marie. That psalmist expressed it so beautifully: "For you formed my inward parts; You covered me in my mother's womb. I will praise You, for I am fearfully and wonderfully made."

What I have learned in these years of loving the Lord and seeking His truth is that joy does not come from material possessions, as wonderful and enjoyable as they may be. Joy does not come from having a wealthy family or a successful career, as much as those things may be desired. Real joy—the kind that lasts forever—comes from trusting in the Lord. Through good times and bad times, sickness and health, we belong to God. He has the ultimate control over what happens to us. He will provide us with a hopeful future.

Life is so precious. I cannot wait to see what His good plans are for me.

With this background, I have had a better appreciation from where I came and what is the purpose of life. As a grandmother, I am able to pass on this knowledge and wisdom to my precious grandchildren. Throughout my whole life, God has opened my eyes and trained me to be a grandmother. Thank You, God, for fearfully and wonderfully making me into the person I am.

72
Grow children with care.

A garden can help people cross generational boundaries. Our grandchildren love to be a part of our garden. The whole process is like a living botany laboratory. And the time we spend together working with soil and plants is a perfect opportunity to act out one of our favorite verses of Scripture: "These words, which I am commanding you today, shall be on your heart. You shall teach them diligently to your sons and shall talk of them when you sit in your house and when you walk by the way and when you lie down and when you rise up" (Deuteronomy 6:6-7 NASB).

We use every opportunity to teach our grandchildren about God and creation. Their little hands help till the ground, scatter the seeds in the trenches, cover the seeds with fertile soil, and help with the first watering. We find that children are perfect for these chores. What child does not love to dig in the dirt?

Each time they visit (which is often, because they live just five minutes away), they cannot get out of the van fast enough to see how the plants are growing. And they can hardly wait for the first harvest. Because there is always more than we need, they get to take some home for their families and also to share with a neighbor.

They share the chores too: weeding, watering, picking snails off plants. We often give them one or more "I was caught being good" stickers to show appreciation for their help. And PaPa's even been known to take them for a special treat at the local yogurt shop or hamburger stand. Our grandchildren have truly bonded with their PaPa by working with him in the yard and the garden.

73
Support your children in their role as parents.

Be an encouragement to your grandchildren's parents today. Find a way to show your support. Compliment them on the way they care for their kids. Attribute the strengths of the grandchildren to the strengths of the parents. Thank the parents for the gift of letting you spend time with the grandkids...for their willingness to share such joy.

If you live close by, offer to watch the kids when you know schedules are tight and the parents could use a break. If you live far away, send money for a babysitter or certificates for a night out. When you focus your attention on the grandkids, you can innocently forget about the simple needs of your children and their spouses. Give them kind words and your approval...not because your approval is required, but because it is appreciated.

74
Share the wisdom of Proverbs.

Like apples of gold in settings of silver is a word spoken in right circumstances. Like an earring of gold and an ornament of fine gold is a wise reprover to a listening ear.

PROVERBS 25:11-12 NASB

Share the wisdom of Proverbs with your grandchildren. Bring a proverb up during a well-suited situation. Tag on a proverb when you send a letter or write a note. Call your grandchildren up with a weekly bit of wisdom. You will be surprised at how quickly they learn these biblical treasures.

> The one who guards his mouth preserves his life;
> the one who opens wide his lips comes to ruin.
>
> PROVERBS 13:3 NASB

> Wisdom is supreme; therefore get wisdom.
> Though it cost all you have, get understanding.
>
> PROVERBS 4:7

> My son, if sinners entice you, do not give in to them.
>
> PROVERBS 1:10

> He who answers before listening—that is his folly and his shame.
>
> PROVERBS 18:13

> Forsake the foolish, and live; and go in the way of understanding.
>
> PROVERBS 9:6 KJV

75
Stay connected with postcards.

One of the pluses of getting older is that we often have more time and money to travel. We also are not restricted only to summer travel. All 12 months are available to pack the old suitcase, and off we go.

Expand the horizons of your grandchildren by introducing them to the places you go. Send postcards depicting skylines, seascapes, monuments, and foreign lands. The grandchildren can learn a lot of geography by looking up the locations on a map.

Here's my method: As we travel in the United States or across the seas, I purchase inexpensive postcards of our favorite sites—historical and cultural—including hotels we stayed in. We place a few of these in my purse and write them while we are having lunch in a café, sitting on a bench in the park, or riding a train through the countryside. We write down information about a special site, a memory, or an event that happened at a specific place. Often we will mention a favorite restaurant that we enjoyed. Of course, a special part of the card is to uplift the family. They love to hear that we miss them and look forward to seeing them when we get back home.

We even mail postcards to our home address. It is fun to receive mail from yourself. These postcards make a wonderful collection of the memories of your trip.

Punch a hole through the upper left-hand corner, thread a colorful ribbon through the holes, tie with a bow, and place the postcards on the coffee table. Your family and friends can easily thumb through these postcards and get a quick overview of your trip.

After the cards are on the coffee table awhile, we untie the ribbon and add them to our scrapbook. On occasion we might place them along with maps and brochures from our journey in an 8½" x 14" manila folder, label the location on the tab, and file everything away in our file cabinet.

76

Quote a quote.

Encourage your grandchildren with quotes of wisdom, humor, and insight. Have one to share with them each time you get together. Make a game of it. See if they can memorize your chosen "quote of the month." Inspire them to search for quotes as well. Encourage them to read books each month and select a quote that speaks to them. And have them write their own! It is amazing how wise a child can be.

These quotes will provide you as grandparents with a resource to plant great thoughts from great men in the minds of young ones. It is amazing how these kernels of truth will provide opportunities for discussion. Here are a few of our favorite quotes:

No one can make you feel inferior without your consent.

ELEANOR ROOSEVELT

When you were born, you cried and the world rejoiced. Live your life in such a manner that when you die the world cries and you rejoice.

OLD INDIAN SAYING

Failure is success if we learn from it.

MALCOMB S. FORBES

Success seems to be largely a matter of hanging on after others have let go.

WILLIAM FEATHER

Never, never, never, never give up.

WINSTON CHURCHILL

77
Let the Lord build your house and your heritage.

Unless the LORD builds the house,
its builders labor in vain.
Unless the LORD watches over the city,
the watchmen stand guard in vain.
In vain you rise early
and stay up late,
toiling for food to eat—
for he grants sleep to those he loves.
Sons are a heritage from the LORD,
children a reward from him.
Like arrows in the hands of a warrior
are sons born in one's youth.
Blessed is the man
whose quiver is full of them.
They will not be put to shame
when they contend with their enemies in the gate.

PSALM 127:1-5

In a recent Bible study that I was in, the teacher asked us, "Did you feel loved by your parents when you were a child?" Many remarked:

"They were too busy for me."

"I spent too much time with the babysitters."

"Dad took us on trips, but he played golf all the time we were away."

"I got in their way. I wasn't important to them."

"Mom was too involved at the country club to spend time with us."

"Mom didn't have to work, but she did just so she wouldn't have to be home with us children."

"A lot of pizzas came to our house on Friday nights when my parents went out for the evening."

I was amazed at how many grown men and women expressed ways they *did not* feel loved in their homes growing up. What would your grandchildren's answers be if someone asked them the same question?

The above Scripture passage gives an overview of what it takes to make and develop a close-knit and healthy family. We first look at the foundation of the home in verse 1: "Unless the LORD builds the house, its builders labor in vain. Unless the LORD watches over the city, the watchmen stand guard in vain."

The protective wall surrounding a city was the very first thing to be constructed when a new city was built. The men of the Old Testament knew they needed protection from the enemy, but they were also smart enough to know that walls could be climbed over, knocked down, or broken apart. Ultimately, the people knew that their real security was the Lord guarding the city.

Today we must return to that trust in the Lord, if we are going to be able to withstand the destruction of our "walls"—the family. As I drive the Southern California freeways, I see parents who are burning the candle at both ends to provide for all the material things they think will make their families happy. We rise early and retire late. In Psalm 127:2, we find this is futile. Our trust must be that the Lord has His hand over our families. The business of our hands is only a futile effort to satisfy those we love.

In verse 3 we see that children are a reward or gift from the Lord. In the Hebrew, *gift* means "property, a possession." Truly, God has loaned us His property or possessions to care for and to enjoy for a certain period of time.

Bob loves to grow vegetables in his raised-bed garden each summer. I am amazed at what it takes to get a good crop. He cultivates the soil, sows seeds, waters, fertilizes, weeds, and prunes. Raising children takes a lot of time, care, nurturing, and cultivating as well. We cannot neglect these responsibilities if we are going to produce good fruit. Left to itself, the garden—and our children—will grow into weeds.

Bob always has a big smile on his face when he brings a large basket full of corn, tomatoes, cucumbers, and beans into the kitchen. As the harvest is Bob's reward, so children are their parents' reward.

Let your home become a garden where the family can thrive and be rejuvenated. Say no when you are tempted to just go through the motions on fast-forward. God has a better plan. He wants you to walk in His ways.

The Legacy
of Love

Love

When Mother Teresa received her Nobel prize, she was asked, "What can we do to promote world peace?" She replied, "Go home and love your family." That is powerful advice for parents and grandparents alike.

Show love to your grandchildren every chance you get. Learn about their lives and what interests them. Your presence in their lives will inspire the legacy of love and the heritage of peace. By becoming involved in a child's life, you take on the responsibility of shepherding him or her toward good choices, meaningful decisions, and fulfilling relationships.

When you are not near your grandchildren, shower them with notes and reminders that you are thinking of them and praying for them. Ask them what they would like to have you pray about. If you start asking this question early in their lives, it will become a comfortable routine. They will feel free to share their requests with you.

There are many simple ways to express your love. You do not have to shower them with lavish gifts. The gift of yourself will be more than enough.

But first you have to give it.

78

Be gentle and loving.

Be completely humble and gentle; be patient, bearing with one another in love.

EPHESIANS 4:2-3

As grandparents, we are at a stage in our lives when we can be gentle giants. Bob can very vividly recall his own grandfather on his father's side of the family. He was known as a very tough disciplinarian when raising Bob's father and his five siblings. However, to Bob's brothers and Bob he was so gentle. He plowed behind a team of mules on his West Texas cotton farm until his mid-seventies. When they were around PaPa, they felt protected and comforted by his presence.

One of the great compliments we can receive is that of being gentle. Paul, Silvanus, and Timothy were compassionate, spiritual mentors to the Thessalonian church. These were very rugged, macho men who were not afraid to be known as gentle warriors. Although they exhibited these gentle traits, they also exhorted, confronted, and admonished the Thessalonians as a father does his children (1 Thessalonians 2:11). While raising our children, my Bob considered himself a very strict father; however, recently our daughter, Jenny, commented that she considered her father to be very gentle. That was a surprise and at the same time a compliment that she thought this about him.

As adults we need gentleness when we teach our children and grandchildren how to reflect God's glory. In the lives of these children we can rejoice when we see where they are spiritually.

A prominent pastor once stated, "Those who minister the gospel should be gentle, tender, and affectionate…what is wrong we should oppose, but it should be in the kindest manner toward those who do wrong."

As we lead with gentleness, we will see those around us gladly respond to our leadership. What a wonderful legacy to leave to our children and grandchildren!

79

Listen.

Concentrate on listening, not speaking. If it is difficult for you to find something to discuss with your grandchild, maybe you are not taking time to listen. Give the discussion some room. Let there be occasional silence. Bring up a topic like school, friends, faith, or a favorite activity, and then rest in the moment for a bit. When children understand your attention is reserved for them, they will open up more and more.

80

"Can't you say it, Grandpa?"

Behold, children are a gift of the LORD.

PSALM 127:3 NASB

"Oh look, Grandpa! I catched it!"

"That's my boy. Now get ready; here comes another. Make me proud and catch this one, too."

"Look, Grandpa! I'm only eight years old, and I can throw faster than anyone in the league!"

"But your batting stinks, Tiger. Can't play in the big leagues if you can't hit."

"Look, Grandpa! I'm 16, and I've already made the varsity team!"

"You'd better do a little less bragging and a little more practicing on your defense. Still needs a lot of work."

"Look, Grandpa! I'm 35, and the company has made me a vice president!"

"Maybe someday you'll start your own business like your old man. Then you'll really feel a sense of accomplishment."

"Look at me, Grandpa! I'm 40, successful, well-respected in the community. I have a wonderful wife and family—aren't you proud of me now, Grandpa? All my life it seems I've caught everything but that one prize I wanted most: your approval. Can't you say it, Grandpa? Is it too much to ask for? Just once I would like to know that feeling every grandchild should have of being loved unconditionally. I would like for you to put your arm around my shoulders and, instead of telling me I'm not good enough, tell me that in your eyes I'm already a winner and always will be no matter what.

"Look at me, Grandpa! I'm all grown up...but in my heart still lives a little boy who yearns for his grandfather's love. Won't you pitch me the words I've waited for all my life?

"I'll catch them, Grandpa. I promise."

Do your grandchildren know you love them? Do they know unconditional acceptance? Are they winners in your eyes? Do they know that? Grandchildren need to know that grandparents really love them. They long to hear us say, "I love you, and I am very proud of you."

81
Embrace the similarities.

Here's my advice: Make sure your children and grand-
children know you love them.

BARBARA BUSH

As we look at today's youth, we might jump to the con-
clusion that they are so very different from those in our
younger days. However, I have learned over the years that
every generation is basically the same, only different. Let
me explain....

Parents are so close to the trees that they cannot see the
forest. They are so close to the children, they are not able
to step back and see that their children are much like themselves. Sure, their hair may be a different color or a different
length. But other than wearing the current fashions, they
are not much different inside from Mom and Dad.

This is where grandparents play a big role. We are able
to step back, become more objective, and give a better perspective on the situation. The grandparent has lived long
enough to have seen it all. We have seen the good and
the bad. We have seen styles and fashions come and go.
We, too, thought that our children were at times irrespon-
sible, strange, and out-to-lunch. We have experienced the
change from impossible to the possible. Generation after
generation has grown into very capable adults, who are
now the parents of their own rascals.

As grandparents, we have observed and know that the
more children change, the more they remain the same. So
grandparents, be encouraged. Your grandchildren inside
have the same desires that you had at their age. These may

be framed differently than when you were a child, but continue to love them through their process of becoming adults.

We as grandparents have a great opportunity to give a better perspective on the situation. After all, we aren't as close to the trees. We have the privilege of seeing more of the forest.

82
Celebrate uniqueness.

For you created my inmost being;
*   you knit me together in my mother's womb.*
I praise you because I am fearfully and wonderfully
*   made;*
*   your works are wonderful,*
*   I know that full well.*
My frame was not hidden from you
*   when I was made in the secret place.*
When I was woven together in the depths of the earth,
*   your eyes saw my unformed body.*
All the days ordained for me
*   were written in your book*
*   before one of them came to be.*

PSALM 139:13-16

Share with your grandchildren how special they are. In a time when there is such pressure to have the perfect body image, do they know they are wonderfully made? Think about each grandchild and focus on his or her uniqueness. As you go through the following activities, take time to notice the special traits, mannerisms, and gifts God gave your grandchildren.

* Write down in your journal the ways your grandchildren are special.

* Take thought of how you will train them based on these differences.

* Learn one new thing about each of your grandchildren today. Do something with that information.

* Praise your grandchild today for being uniquely made.

83

Plan ahead.

But seek first his kingdom and his righteousness, and all these things will be given to you as well.

MATTHEW 6:33

We have some dear friends in Arizona who were very future-oriented about their high school daughter's "someday wedding." They knew it would be a long time in the future, but why procrastinate?

Their plan was very simple: They and a few of their friends would save their pennies for buying their daughter's future wedding dress. Who ever heard of purchasing an expensive wedding dress for a penny? People won't even stop to pick up a lost penny on the sidewalk. How can a penny buy a wedding dress?

You cannot believe what has happened. Over the years, friends got behind their endeavor and faithfully set aside all those good-for-nothing pennies. We helped roll those coins into their paper wrappers and stored them away in a secret hiding place in the kitchen pantry. Little pennies added together take up a lot of space and are very heavy.

Then one spring, their daughter and future son-in-law announced that they were to be married the following January. At last the big day approached. Her parents had big plans for those pennies. This huge load of pennies was rolled into the bank, with a local photographer and newspaper writer standing by to write up this special interest story.

The approximate calculation? Because our friends planned ahead, one thousand dollars of pennies would be deposited to the wedding dress account.

You can really buy a wedding dress for a penny.

Think about ways to plan ahead for your grandchildren's lives. You can save up family photos. Keep your journal up-to-date and save that as a treasury of memories for the child. There are many ways to show your love as time passes.

84

Be a granddaughter's example of love.

God borrows from many creatures to make a little girl. He uses the song of a bird, the squeal of a pig, the stubbornness of a mule, the antics of a monkey, the spryness of a grasshopper, the curiosity of a cat, the speed of a gazelle, the slyness of a fox, the softness of a kitten, and to top it all off, He adds the mysterious mind of a woman.

ALAN BECK

Grandchildren—little granddaughters in particular—are the nicest things that happen to grandfathers. Girls are born with a little bit of angel shine about them and, though it wears thin sometimes, there is always enough left to laser your heart—even when they are sitting in the mud, crying temperamental tears, or parading up the street in Grandma's best clothes.

Along with their father, we grandfathers have a tremendous responsibility to keep our little girls on the right track. No other part of society has as much influence on our girls as we do. Our daughters and granddaughters want us to be leaders of our home. They are finding in us the qualities they will someday look for in a husband. They need to discover how a man thinks about life, and how we administer and delegate certain job responsibilities to the family team.

As adult males, we are the most important men in our young lady's life. She will build her life based on what she sees in her grandpa and her father.

85

Pass the buck.

Money talks. Our money and how we use it speak volumes about our life, our priorities, and our view of God's provision. Make arrangements to include your grandchildren in your inheritance.

The way you interact with your grandchildren over the years will give them a rich inheritance of love. By also offering them part of your financial heritage, you offer them some stability—perhaps the means to finance a current need or a lifelong dream. The money might be what makes the difference between their family just getting by and living securely.

> If you believe in something, you support it. If you support something, the time comes when good wishes and cordial words are not enough and your hand reaches for your pocketbook. Then the fun begins. For giving is fun. If you refuse to give, your support is wavering; and if your support wavers, it can't be that you believe in that something in any strong way. Maybe our account books, after all, offer the honest list of those things in which we really believe.
>
> KENNETH IRVING BROWN

86

Practice the art of good grandparenting.

But everyone must be quick to hear, slow to speak, and slow to anger.

JAMES 1:19 NASB

Our goal as grandparents is to bring out the very best in our grandchildren. To be effective, we need to show our grandchildren that we really care for them—not just in words, but also in actions. Through their music, friends, clothes, and grades, they are continually asking, "Do you really love me?"

As grandparents we can show we care when we:

- Really listen—turn off the TV and put down the newspaper or magazine.

- Take an interest in them as people.

- Be clear in your expectations.

- Share your knowledge with them.

- Reinforce positive behavior and discourage unacceptable behavior.

- Trust them to fulfill their promises.

- Be flexible and open to new ideas.

- Have a good sense of humor.

- Set standards that raise and challenge their standards.

- Set the stage for the direction of the family unit.

Remember, we are not the parents, but we can set the tone for teaching our grandchildren. As the respected grandparents, we are in a very enviable position. The kids love to work along with Grandma and Grandpa, and you have more influence than you will ever know. Respect that position of praise.

Grandchildren are bountiful blessings to the grandparents who, without direct parental control, can usually enjoy their offspring at a safe distance. Herein, we explore the joys of observing, teaching and loving the children's children. May they live happily ever after.

DR. CRISWELL FREEMAN

There are many who want me to tell them of secret ways of becoming perfect and I can only tell them that the sole secret is a hearty love of God, and the only way of attaining that love is by loving. You learn to speak by speaking, to study by studying, to run by running, to work by working; and just so you learn to love God and man by loving. Begin as a mere apprentice and the very power of love will lead you on to become a master of the art.

ST. FRANCIS DE SALES

87

Gather together.

There is no spectacle on earth more appealing than that of a beautiful woman in the act of cooking dinner for someone she loves.

THOMAS WOLFE

What is the difference between a house and a home? We hear people interchange these two words as being the same. But those of us who are fortunate to live in a home know the difference. Home is not simply four walls with a roof overhead. It is not just a structure in an upscale neighborhood. (In fact, many homes are found in the poorer neighborhoods of a city.) It doesn't have to have a certain architecture or style of construction (many are just plain homes—nothing fancy).

Home is a state of mind, built with more than bricks and mortar—always with a lot of love. The collective size of the hearts of the people inside is more important than the size of the building.

A home is a place where we know we are protected and loved. It is a place where freedom rings. The occupants do not have to be molded out of the same cookie cutter. Each person is encouraged to grow in his or her own directions for life. In this place called home, we can all cry when we are sad and laugh with shouts of joy when we have victories.

This wonderful haven called home is a place where we gather together to celebrate life. Traditions are carried on, parties are held to celebrate special kinds of events, and food flows as much as love. When the children leave home, they are always glad to come back home.

88
Follow the perfect manual.

But where can wisdom be found? And where is the place of understanding?

JOB 28:12 NASB

My friend Florence Littauer wrote a book titled *Looking for Love in All the Wrong Places.* And it is true. We look for love in all the wrong places. We seek wisdom in places where there is no wisdom by talking to friends, reading magazines, listening to talk shows, and attending seminars. We live in a culture that has a difficult time reading the instruction manual. For some reason, we want to invent the wheel by ourselves. We have trouble seeking the truth from the wise.

The writer of the book of Job struggled with knowing what to do. In Job 28:12 he asked, "Where can wisdom be found?" All through chapter 28, he searched for the answer:

- Man does not know its value (verse 13)
- It is not found in the land of the living (verse 13)
- The inner earth says, "It is not in me" (verse 14)
- The sea says, "It is not with me" (verse 14)
- You cannot buy it with gold or silver (verse 15)
- Precious stones do not have it (verse 16)
- It cannot be equated with gold (verse 17)
- Pearls do not have it (verse 18)
- It is hidden from the eyes of all living creatures (verse 21)
- God understands its way, and He knows its place (verse 23)
- God looks to the ends of the earth and sees everything under heaven (verse 24)
- God saw wisdom and declared it (verse 27)
- God established it and searched it out (verse 27)

Job and his friends claimed wisdom of themselves, but wisdom is clearly an outgrowth of God and not merely something to be obtained. Although we can know and understand many things, we cannot attain the level of Creator wisdom. There will always be questions that only God can answer. Solomon knew that true wisdom is not found in human understanding but is from God alone (see Proverbs 1:7).

Share this wisdom with your grandchildren. And when they have questions, direct them back to God's perfect manual: Scripture.

89
Pray for your family.

Lord, behold our family
We thank You for this place in which we dwell,
For the love that unites us,
For the peace accorded us this day,
For the hope with which we expect the morrow;
For the health, the work, the food,
The bright skies
That make our lives delightful;
For our friends in all parts of the earth. Amen.

ROBERT LOUIS STEVENSON

Pray this prayer for your family all week. Really take time to thank the Lord for the love, peace, hope, and health you are experiencing. See the reflection of God's delight in the eyes of your family. Encourage a sense of hope by modcling your trust in the Lord, even during uncertain times—especially in uncertain times.

Choose a prayer, like the one above by Robert Louis Stevenson, or maybe one that has been a tradition in your family, and write it out and place it by your main door. As you enter or exit your home, honor God by praying for the family He has given to you.

90

Accept the reward of grandchildren.

Sons are a heritage from the LORD, children a reward from him.

PSALM 127:3

Our grandchildren are continually reaching out to see if Mom and Dad and Grandma and Grandpa really love them. They will continue to test their parents and grandparents until they hear *and* believe the words "We love you no matter what" even when they:

+ yell and scream in the grocery store

+ have temper tantrums in the restaurant

+ wear strange clothes

+ get funny haircuts in odd colors

+ use vulgar language

+ run away from home

+ get bad grades in school

+ run around with friends that we do not approve of

In these unacceptable behaviors, they are indirectly asking, "Do you approve of me?" And they are not hearing our response.

We had a good friend whose son was not into sports and athletics like his dad desired. He was into motocross racing. The parents came to our pastor, and the dad asked the pastor what he should do. The pastor, not surprisingly, said, "Take up motocrossing!" The dad predictably said, "I don't like dirt, grease, or motorcycles."

The pastor replied, "How much do you love your son? Enough to get grease on your hands and clothes?" The next week Dad was off with his son to the local motocross event. Soon after that the dad was involved with dirt, grease, and different people. Through these actions the father showed his son that he loved him more than anything else.

We need to understand that our grandsons and granddaughters are a heritage from the Lord, and that all children are a reward from God. And we need to start living as though we believe it. If you have resisted connecting with a grandchild because of your personal list of reasons, review that list again. Is having your way more important than sharing a life with a child?

91
Write on.

Write your grandchildren a note letting them know how much you love them. Give a few specific traits you like about them. Even young children love the thrill of receiving mail.

Buy postcards from your hometown and have them stamped and ready to go. When you think about a child or see something you want to share with him or her, write it and send it!

Take advantage of the wonders of e-mail. A correspondence relationship can start up easily via the Internet.

When you send a note, mark the date on your calendar. Then when a month goes by, write on.

92
Walk together in wisdom.

For he will not often consider the years of his life, because
God keeps him occupied with the gladness of his heart.
ECCLESIASTES 5:20 NASB

As grandparents, we walk into the golden years and find out that they are not so golden. Where your mirror and photographs were once your friends, you now realize they have become your enemies. The person you see in the mirror looks more like your parent, and that is one person you never wanted to favor. Where you used to find yourself in the photo, you now do not even want a picture taken—no more mirrors and no more photographs.

One of the great values of these golden years is that we have senior citizen discounts in all areas of life, we can belong to AARP, and we qualify for Social Security and Medicare.

Along with the good, we have to put up with comments like:

- Let me help you with your bag.
- Should we take the elevator to the second floor?
- Be careful when you step off the curb.

It makes you feel like you are still in kindergarten, and it is difficult to find your place in the world around you.

Who and what are the persons God wants us to be at this stage of our lives? As grandparents who are senior citizens, we have wanted to pursue what God has for us right at this moment. Except for the mirror and photographs, we have not felt better in years. We are eager to take on the world (at least we have opinions on everything). We are more able to take on the giants of life, because God keeps us occupied with gladness of heart.

We have the opportunity to be an encouragement to those all around us. People want to have us share some of the secrets of contentment. Being grandparents gives us an opportunity to really shape the next generation. Our love, our connection, our encouragements, our support cannot be delivered by anyone but us. The gladness in our hearts is what makes today so much fun. We can hardly wait to get out of bed to see what God has in store for us.

93

Always mean always.

Love is patient, love is kind. It does not envy, it does not boast, it is not proud. It is not rude, it is not self-seeking, it is not easily angered, it keeps no record of wrongs. Love does not delight in evil but rejoices with the truth. It always protects, always trusts, always hopes, always perseveres.

1 CORINTHIANS 13:4-7

It is very hard for us mere mortals to adequately understand the word *always*. In today's culture, we do not adequately understand this kind of commitment. When we say *always,* don't we usually mean "sometimes"…or "most of the time"? But *always* really means "eternal" and "everlasting." Can anyone commit to *always*?

When Scripture says *always*, it means "always, never-changing, dependable until death." We as grandparents are challenged when Paul writes that love always protects, trusts, hopes, and perseveres.

As grandparents, we so want our family to honor us with this kind of love. We also want to be known to honor and respect them with the same intensity of love. When Grandpa or Grandma says something, you can take it to the bank. We want to be known as people who do what they say they are going to do—not sometimes, but *always*.

As we become older and look back over life's journey, may we know that love and what it encompasses is indeed the true victory of life.

I love you today, where you are and as you are.
You do not have to be anything but what you are

for me to love you. I love you now; not sometime when you are worthy, but today when you may need love most.

I will not withhold my love or withdraw it. There are no strings on my love, no price. I will not force it upon you when you are not ready. It is just there, freely offered with both hands.

Take what you want today. The more you take, the more there is. It is good if you can return love; but if you cannot today, that is all right too. Love is its own joy. Bless me by letting me love you today.

AUTHOR UNKNOWN

94

Be a giver.

For all things come from You, and from Your hand we have given You.

1 CHRONICLES 29:14 NASB

Being a giver is much more rewarding than to be a taker of a gift. There is seldom a time when we receive a gift, other than on special occasions. When we have the opportunity to be with our grandchildren, we are able to give—to give and to give—*love*. What a joy to give them love!

Just imagine what a heavy schedule of appointments President Abraham Lincoln had to keep day after day. Yet, when an elderly grandmother with no official business in mind asked to see him, he graciously consented.

As she entered Lincoln's office, he rose to greet her and asked how he might be of service. She replied that she had not come to ask a favor. She had heard that the president liked a certain kind of cookie, so she had baked some for him and brought them to his office.

With tears in his eyes, Lincoln responded, "You are the very first person who has ever come into my office asking not, expecting not, but rather bringing me a gift. I thank you from the bottom of my heart."

I know I get so excited when my children and grandchildren give me a gift, not a request. How much more must God rejoice when we do not bring a list of requests, but instead we simply bring Him the gift of our gratitude and love. Nothing pleases our heavenly Father more than our sincere thanksgiving.

95
Raise healthy grandchildren.

By wisdom a house is built, and through understanding it is established; through knowledge its rooms are filled with rare and beautiful treasures.

PROVERBS 24:3-4

There are three magic words in raising children and hopefully the next generation of grandchildren. After all, we are not raising just one generation. No matter how involved we want to be in raising our children's children, we will have a great impact on their lives. Why? Because our children will most likely raise their children (your grandchildren) how they were raised. These three magic words are:

* wisdom

* understanding

* knowledge

When we use these three magic words, our rooms are filled with rare and beautiful treasures—children who are obedient, polite, considerate, good citizens, and who honor God. What parent or grandparent would not love to have these treasures?

When we are out in public and observe a healthy, functioning family, we know that they directly or indirectly have been observing these three important guidelines. How do we know that? Because we can see the rewards and/or blessings of that training. The parents have rare and beautiful treasures. Is it easy to be blessed? No! It takes a lot of work and stick-to-it discipline to have these treasures. You have to believe in the end results. We always go up to the parents of well-mannered children and compliment them on their efforts. When you see something good, shout it from the housetops!

Use the time you are with your treasured grandchildren as an opportunity to teach. You do not have to be preachy or stern. The teaching can be in a real, live situation. Many times these children will listen to you before they will listen to their own parents. You have a great deal of influence, so do not be afraid to use your adult status with these little ones.

96
Sacrifice.

You also, as living stones, are being built up as a spiritual house for a holy priesthood, to offer up spiritual sacrifices acceptable to God through Jesus Christ.

1 PETER 2:5 NASB

A man touring a rural area of the Far East saw a boy pulling a crude plow while an old man held the handles and guided it through the rice paddy. The visitor commented, "I suppose they are very poor."

"Yes," said his guide. "When their church was built, they wanted to give something to help, but they had no money. So they sold their only ox."

In America we may not have to give up an ox and pull the plow ourselves, but there are many ways we can give. I am always amazed when I go out to a job site and see pallet after pallet of bricks and stones. They are just sitting there, not much beauty to them at all. But when I go back in a few weeks, I am startled by what the skilled mason has done with those stones. They have become fireplaces, ornamental decorations for homes, retaining walls, and walkways.

God wants to make a "spiritual house" from all of our "living stones." Some spiritual sacrifices for the transformation will be costly, but what is gained by our giving—God's praise—is always greater than what we give. The time you take, the commitments you make for your grandchildren, will create the legacy of a spiritual house for your family.

97

Feel free to cry.

But we proved to be gentle among you, as a nursing mother tenderly cares for her own children.

1 THESSALONIANS 2:7 NASB

When you think of the apostle Paul, you may think of the person who endured imprisonment, flogging, stoning, and shipwrecks (see 2 Corinthians 11:23-27), and that toughness was very much a part of the fiery apostle. But today's reading reveals his tender side. He describes himself as being gentle and tender. His hard-as-nails toughness did not mean he was without his soft side.

I saw an example of a tough-but-tender man when Barbara Walters interviewed real-life hero "Stormin' Norman" Schwarzkopf, the four-star general who led the allied forces of Desert Storm to their Gulf War victory over Iraq. As this tough military man talked about the war, I saw tears in his eyes.

His interviewer noticed, too, and in her classic style, Barbara Walters asked, "Why, General, aren't you afraid to cry?" Schwarzkopf replied without hesitation, "No, Barbara, I'm afraid of a man who won't cry!" This truly great man knows that being tough does not mean being insensitive or unfeeling or afraid to cry. No wonder soldiers gave their best when they served under his command. They knew the general cared about them; they could trust the man giving the orders. Men want leaders whose hearts can be touched by their situations and who touch their hearts as well.

Even today I vividly remember the encouragement that my high school and college basketball coaches would give me when they called me to the sidelines. As the coach explained the next play or the strategy for the game-winning maneuver, he would put his arm on my shoulder. That simple touch said, "Bob, I believe in you. You can make it happen."

Athletics can indeed be a real source of encouragement as boys travel the path to manhood. Granted, professional sports have become larger than life with the influx of the media dollars, but athletics remains a place where we can see the tender side of a tough athlete. That is what we are looking at when we see grown men jump into the arms of a coach or a teammate, two or more buddies high-fiving it, or a swarm of players jumping on top of the player who just made the big play. This childlike excitement is the tender side of the not-to-be-beaten athlete.

Are you able to give your grandchildren pats on the back or bear hugs? We are all on the same team—God's—and we all need some encouragement as we head onto the field to make the big plays. We need each other if we are going to be victorious in this game called life.

98
Be a loving listener.

When there are many words, transgression is unavoidable, but he who restrains his lips is wise.

PROVERBS 10:19 NASB

I have heard it said that God gave us two ears and only one mouth because He wants us to listen twice as much as we speak. I do not know about you, but I have never had to apologize for something I have not said. It is much easier and really more natural for us to speak rather than to listen. Speaking comes naturally. We have to learn to listen. It takes real discipline to keep from talking.

As parents—and certainly as grandparents—we need to be known as good listeners. And while you listen, be sure to remember there are always two sides of every story. At the time, you are only hearing one version of what happened. Postpone any judgment until you have heard all the evidence—then wait some more.

Eleanor Roosevelt, in one of her many speeches, states,

> A mature person is one who does not think only in absolutes, who is able to be objective even when deeply stirred emotionally, who has learned that there is both good and bad in all people and in all things, and who walks humbly and deals charitably with the circumstances of life. Knowing that in this world no one is all knowing and therefore all of us need both love and charity.

Our Scripture verse talks to us about being more of a listener than a talker. Too many words can lead to putting one's foot into one's mouth. The more we speak, the greater the chance of being offensive. The wise person will restrain his speech. Listening seldom gets us into trouble, but our mouths certainly cause transgressions.

When listening to our grandchildren, they will tell us everything on their own (that is also true regarding all people). People love to talk, and when they do, you hear sometimes more than you want to hear. By the time we are grandparents, it is easier to listen. Grandchildren love to talk to their grandparents because they feel secure and safe around you. Do not violate that trust. Once violated, it is hard to regain.

99
Adopt a grandchild.

We live in an age of latchkey children. For various reasons, children arrive home from school and Mom and/or Dad are not home for a few more hours. Many seniors live away from their immediate families and are not able to see their children and grandchildren on a regular basis. These two conditions in today's society give us an opportunity to adopt several children in the neighborhood as grandchildren. There are many activities you can do to enrich the children in your church and neighborhood:

- Establish a day and time and host a story hour when you can read good literature to them.

- Show a preselected video that teaches good values, then follow up with a discussion about what was being taught.

- Expose your new grandchildren to basic cooking skills, leading to their ability to care for themselves when their parents are away.

- Invite a fireman/policeman in to talk about safety around the home.

- Have a tea party for the young girls and a cookout for the young boys.

- Instruct the youngsters on how to operate the dishwasher, washing machine, dryer, and even how to fold and iron clothes.

- Do a session on basic manners, role-play how to talk on the phone, how to introduce one to another, how to set the table, etc.

100
Make someone feel special!

Finally, we have many beautiful memories of our "You Are Special Today" plate—an old American tradition that is a relatively new one in our family. We often bring this bright red plate out at dinnertime to celebrate special people who sit at our table.

When our grandson Chad was six, he created a new twist to the red plate. We had set it at PaPa Bob's place to honor his birthday. Chad exclaimed, "Let's all go around and tell PaPa why we think he's special." So we did. What a great idea!

The next week the grandchildren came for dinner, and Chad said, "Grammy Em, let's use the special red plate at dinner." I said, "Great! Whom should we honor tonight?" "How about me?" he said. We all honored Chad that evening, and we went around and told Chad how special he was. Then he said, "Now I want to tell you why *I* think I'm special. I think I am special because I'm a child of God."

This began yet another new tradition for the red plate. It has helped us celebrate how special we are not only to other people and ourselves, but also to the Lord, who created us and gave us eternal life. It reminds us that we are sons and daughters of the living God.

The grandchildren's eyes light up when we honor them on various days and events of celebration.

101
Take the time.

Finally, you are bombarded by "How come?" "Why, Grandma?" "What does this mean, Grandpa?" don't wave away the questions with the flick of your hand or put off an answer until "another time." Make these questions come to life. If it is something the parent should address, then discuss that and why. But if it is a way for you to share God's patience, wisdom, and desire for young minds to grow, then ignore your plan for the day. Perhaps taking time to visit with your grandchild or assuage a child's fear or concern *is* what God has planned for your day.

Take on these "How come?" interruptions. Over time, you will replace a child's anxious questions with the assurance of God's love—and, really, what could be better!

> Nobody can do for little children what grandparents do. Grandparents sort of sprinkle stardust over the lives of little children.
>
> ALEX HALEY

Books by
Bob and Emilie Barnes

**Books by
Bob & Emilie Barnes**

*Minute Meditations
for Couples*

*A Little Book of Manners
for Boys*

Abundance of the Heart

*15-Minute Devotions
for Couples*

Books by Emilie Barnes

The 15-Minute Organizer

15 Minutes Alone with God

*15 Minutes of Peace
with God*

101 Ways to Lift Your Spirits

*The Busy Woman's Guide
to Healthy Eating*

Cleaning Up the Clutter

A Tea to Comfort Your Soul

A Cup of Hope

*Emilie's Creative
Home Organizer*

*Everything I Know
I Learned in My Garden*

Fill My Cup, Lord

Friends Are a Blessing

Friends of the Heart

*A Grandma Is a
Gift from God*

Help Me Trust You, Lord

If Teacups Could Talk

An Invitation to Tea

Join Me for Tea

A Journey Through Cancer

*Keep It Simple
for Busy Women*

Let's Have a Tea Party!

A Little Book of Manners

*Minute Meditations
for Busy Moms*

*Minute Meditations
for Women*

More Hours in My Day

Safe in the Father's Hands

*Strength for Today,
Bright Hope for Tomorrow*

Survival for Busy Women

*The Twelve Teas®
of Celebration*

*The Twelve Teas®
of Christmas*

*The Twelve Teas®
of Friendship*

Books by Bob Barnes

*15 Minutes Alone with God
for Men*

Minute Meditations for Men

*What Makes a Man
Feel Loved*

**HARVEST HOUSE
PUBLISHERS**